WHO ON EARTH IS GOD?

WHO ON EARTH IS GOD?

Making Sense of God in the Bible

NEIL RICHARDSON

Bloomsbury Academic
An imprint of Bloomsbury Publishing Plc

B L O O M S B U R Y
LONDON • NEW DELHI • NEW YORK • SYDNEY

Bloomsbury Academic
An imprint of Bloomsbury Publishing Plc

50 Bedford Square	1385 Broadway
London	New York
WC1B 3DP	NY 10018
UK	USA

www.bloomsbury.com

BLOOMSBURY and the Diana logo are trademarks of Bloomsbury Publishing Plc

First published 2014
Reprinted by Bloomsbury Academic 2014, 2015

British Library Cataloguing-in-Publication Data
A catalogue record for this book is available from the British Library.

ISBN: HB:	978-0-56706-675-6
PB:	978-0-56747-243-4
ePDF:	978-0-56746-601-3
ePub:	978-0-56753-813-0

Library of Congress Cataloging-in-Publication Data
A catalogue record for this book is available from the Library of Congress.

Typeset by Forthcoming Publications (www.forthpub.com)
Printed and bound in Great Britain

For Donald Eadie,
Colleague, Mentor, Friend

Contents

Foreword

I am writing this book both for those who would call themselves Christians and those who would not. Many in both those groups find the Bible difficult and obscure, and that is hardly surprising. The Bible has many critics; some of its stories and teaching and much of its language are alien to most contemporary cultures. I hope that readers unfamiliar with the Bible will not be put off by the many biblical references in this book. It's not necessary to look them all up to follow the argument.

In this age of globalization, I believe that the Bible is a book whose time has finally come. Its cosmic perspectives, for example, with the threat of climate change and international conflict, are more significant than ever. I write also in the conviction that the question of God — God's reality, character and purpose — is the most important question which the Church and the wider world face today. It's the most important question any of us can wrestle with. Yet some of the Bible's images and stories of God are very difficult.

Apart from the Bible, many people today struggle with the very concept of 'God': who, or what, are we talking about? Best-selling books like Richard Dawkins' *The God Delusion* have poured scorn on the whole idea of a supernatural being. But, as I shall ask in this book, is that the right way to think of God?

The Church both hinders and helps. At its worst, the Church makes it more difficult for people to believe in God; at its best, it begins to make belief in God both attractive and credible. So perhaps I should 'confess' to being a minister of the British Methodist Church, and hope that this confession will not deter would-be readers. (A brief 'personal postscript' at the end of the book may be where some readers would like to start).

I am grateful to a number of people for reading and commenting on drafts of various chapters: my wife, Rhiannon, my sons Mark, James and Simon, Old Testament scholars Dr Adrian Curtis and the Rev Dr Michael Thompson, Dr Stanley Pearson, a member of my former church in Leeds, Edith Blair and Maurice and Brenda Coleman, members of the church I now attend in Ludlow, England.

I owe a special word of thanks to the Rev. Kerry Tankard, who read a draft of the whole book, and offered many valuable suggestions.

These and many other people have helped to keep my feet more on the ground than they would otherwise have been. It's presumptuous of anyone to try to write a book about God. No-one can write objectively. It is, or ought to be, a searching experience. Certainly, I have found it so.

In writing this book, I have been conscious of our world's multiple crises: crises of faith, poverty and hunger, international conflict, climate change, the restlessness of societies 'rich in things but poor in soul' - and many more. So this book is anything but an 'academic' exercise. In the end, belief in God is a practical matter, or it is nothing.

Introduction

I never understood quite what was meant by 'God'
EDWARD THOMAS[1]

Children's Letters to God has long been a favourite book of mine. A letter I particularly like in the section called 'The Critics', is the angry one from 'Raymond':

> Dear God,
>> I got left back.
> Thanks a lot,
>> Raymond.

These young critics have their own suggestions to make to God; for example,

> Dear God,
>> Are you real? Some people don't not [*sic*] believe it. If you are you'd better do something quick.
>> Harriet Ann.[2]

The trouble is: God doesn't. So, God has plenty of older critics as well. Richard Dawkins, author of best-selling *The God Delusion*, has argued that it's time for the human race to leave behind infantile concepts such as 'god'; it goes with belief in the tooth fairy or in Santa Claus. Yet a

church leader in Britain, speaking a few years ago on the radio, said he
didn't believe in the god Dawkins rejects. So what is going on? We might
well ask: who on earth is God?

1. God and the Bible

'God' is a very strange word. It's a swear word — as in 'My God!' It's a
word which sometimes begins with a capital letter and sometimes
doesn't; if you think your 'god' is the only god, you're likely to write
'God', not 'god'. But to what does this strange word 'god' refer? Unlike all
the animate and inanimate objects we can see around us, God can't be
seen. Even with abstract ideas and organizations, we can usually say what
they mean: 'patriotism', 'the European Union', and so on. But God? God
is not at all obvious.

A Problem God?

Many religious people, including Christians, think they know the answer
to the question. But Bishop John Taylor, writing in the early 1990s,
expressed surprise 'that so few religious people ever stop and think about
God. The thought of him may be often in their minds, but they do not
explore it. It does not grow, is not allowed to change'.[3]

Is he right? In Britain I have heard people say that God is talked about
more in the pubs than in the churches. An exaggeration, perhaps, but the
silence about God in the churches is often deafening. Or else, talk about
God is a little too self-confident, and that is troubling as well. The Bible
suggests more than once that 'God has a healthy mistrust for his more
self-assured supporters'.[4]

A Problem Bible?

It's not just God who is the problem. So is the Bible. We need to do some serious re-thinking about the Bible, too. What are we to make of it? Did God really say and do all that the Bible claims he said and did? If he did, is he credible? And if he didn't say and do all those things, then is the Bible credible? Is anything left of its supposed authority and inspiration?

Many Christians these days, especially in so-called developed countries, are quite ignorant of the Bible. We turn a blind eye to God's violent behaviour in the Bible, or are surprisingly relaxed about it. Not so the newcomer to church who heard a sermon about God striking down a man misguided enough to touch the ark of the covenant (1 Samuel 6.6-7). That newcomer to church vowed never to return.

Richard Dawkins, admittedly, directs his fire at easy targets such as dysfunctional religion and biblical fundamentalism. But it is not always clear what alternatives are on offer. For example, what sort of God do we get if the Bible is read less literally and more imaginatively and less woodenly? Or are we 'allowed' to read it more selectively? But then we should need to ask: on what basis do we make our selection? Surely something a bit more substantial than 'My favourite bits are...'

Objections to God

God is the object of faith and belief for millions of people. God, of course, can be a mystery — perhaps should be — to people with faith, as well as to people without faith. But God can be so much of a mystery that many wonder whether he actually exists. But if God does, that only seems to add to our problems. Think of the earthquake in Haiti, the child dying of cancer, the Holocaust of World War II...; if the Creator of all is responsible for these things, surely he cannot be a loving creator, or else that creator cannot be almighty.

To make matters worse, religious people across the world (Christians not excluded) commit acts of violence in the name of their god. Other agents and influences in the world promote human wellbeing, or, at least, many try to do so; religion often appears to do the opposite. Devout people and their religion are not always the best advert for God. Nor — if Richard Dawkins is to be believed — is the Bible.

Objections to the Bible

In *The God Delusion* Dawkins describes the God of the Old Testament as 'arguably the most unpleasant character in all fiction'.[5] Christopher Hitchens, author of *God Is Not Great*, is of a similar mind. There is certainly a case to answer. The Bible seems to be a mixed blessing; it both attracts and alienates, and that is also true of its God. So, in trying to make sense of God in the Bible (our subtitle), we shall have to address the sharp criticisms made about the Bible and its God.

Stories about the violence of God tend to be airbrushed out of increasingly bland, contemporary versions of Christian faith and of the lectionaries — the passages appointed to be read in many churches each Sunday. But even Christians familiar with the Bible's more difficult passages seem remarkably relaxed about them. Many seem to have no problem with attributing acts of violence and destruction to God. Biblical scholars occasionally try to justify them with rather feeble explanations; for example, God wiped out the Canaanites in the book of Joshua 'with a heavy heart'. Discrediting God in order to champion a certain view of the Bible's authority seems an odd way for a Christian to proceed.

This book calls for serious re-thinking about God and the God of the Bible — especially in the churches. It is urgently needed in a fast-changing world. What we believe about God can't be somehow ring-fenced from what is going on around us. If it is, it will rapidly become meaningless — or as relevant as a child's comfort blanket. So we need to ask: are there still grounds for saying that God exists? If there are, is God still credible? Do we need to interpret differently the ways in which the Bible portrays God? But before we come to these questions, we look at the words 'atheist' and 'atheism'. Their meaning is not as straightforward as it first appears.

2. 'There Is No God'?

If you look at the section in a bookshop marked 'religion' these days, you may well find books by atheists such as Richard Dawkins' *The God Delusion* or Christopher Hitchens' *God Is Not Great.* There have been other books with eye-catching titles, such as *God's Funeral*, by A.N. Wilson (though Wilson himself is not an atheist). But at the outset of our discussion we need to face the atheist's claim: 'There is no God'.

What is Atheism?

The Bible appears to give atheists short shrift:

> Fools say in their heart, 'There is no God' (Psalm 14.1a CEB).

The Psalmist goes on to say of these 'fools':

> They are corrupt and do evil things;
>
> Not one of them does anything good (v.4).

The words jar in a mostly tolerant culture like ours. But, like most verses in the Bible, here are two we should not simply take at face value. This is not because we are rejecting the authority of the Bible — I come later to that question — it's because these words, like all the Bible's words, were first spoken, and eventually written down in a culture very different from ours.

So, we have to ask what kind of 'atheist' the Psalmist was talking about. Is he implying, as a modern commentator suggests, that the doing of evil in his situation 'equals practical atheism' and that this atheism is a form of 'egocentricity'? That may be true of what atheism amounted to in practice then. But many readers of this book will know atheists who seems anything but 'corrupt', self-centred and doers of 'evil things'.

Rowan Williams, former archbishop of Canterbury, suggests that '"atheism" may be a less simple idea than either its defenders or its attackers assume':[6] 'If we want to understand an atheist and his atheism, we need to know which god he is rejecting and why'. So, what is an atheist denying? Is it not so obvious after all?

Christian Atheists?

When I took pastoral charge of a church in Leeds in the UK in 2001, two or three regular attenders told me they were atheists. As I got to know them, I discovered two things: they had indeed rejected traditional Christian understandings of God, but, secondly, they were more Christian in character than many people who do believe in God. Were they mistaken about the beliefs they rejected? If they rejected the God of the Bible about whom Dawkins and Hitchens are so vitriolic, we might have some sympathy with them. After all, even the God who answers prayers in the Bible poses awkward questions for us today, like the prophet Elijah who prayed for a drought, and there was one (James 5.17). Or is Dawkins, in criticizing the God of the Bible, being as literalist as the religious people of whom he is so critical? Was this the God (or 'god'?) rejected by the atheists in my church congregation?

I am not suggesting that an atheist might not be an atheist after all. That would be presumptuous and patronising. But I am saying that if a person says 'I don't believe in God', having in mind a 'god' which does not correspond to 'God' at all (supposing 'God' really exists), that statement needn't be the end of the conversation. Some atheists are atheists because they reject concepts of God which they consider to be incredible or subchristian or both. And they may well be right. But are there other options — especially if we reject some traditional understandings of the Bible?

In an autobiographical introduction to one of her earlier books, Karen Armstrong relates how she outgrew her childhood ideas of God. She claims that her experience of God was not unusual, arguing that 'each generation has to create the image of God that works for them'. That last point seems to me to concede rather too much to post-modernism: in effect, 'choose the god that's right for you'. But she is surely right to ask 'Is modern atheism a similar denial of a "god" which is no longer adequate to the problems of our time?'[7]

So, at the outset, I suggest, we need to query a 'description' of God which is common amongst both religious and non-religious people. This is the description of God as 'a supernatural being'. The word 'super-natural' doesn't occur in the Bible, and it won't help us in understanding or interpreting the Bible. But I am more concerned here with the other two words: '*a being*'. God is not a being alongside or above other beings. A god so described is simply too small: a god maybe, but not *God*. God is the ultimate, mysterious reality 'in whom we live and move and have our being'. Even if we make him (and this kind of god usually is masculine) the biggest being by far, that still leaves him as a god, not *God*.

3. God and gods

A Question of Justice

In the Bible, Psalm 82 offers an intriguing contrast between God and lesser gods:

> God has taken his place in the divine council;
> in the midst of the gods he holds judgement:
> How long will you judge unjustly
> and show partiality to the wicked? (vv.1-2).

God's indictment of 'the gods' continues in verses 3 and 4: they should give justice to the weak and the orphan, the lowly and the destitute, rescuing them from 'the wicked'.

After these words from 'God', the Psalmist goes on to say this about 'the gods':

> They have neither knowledge nor understanding,
> they walk around in darkness;
> all the foundations of the earth are shaken (v.5).

The Psalm declares the doom of these gods — 'You shall die' (v.6) — and prays for the vindication of the real God (v.8).

So, the Bible itself invites us to critique the word 'god'; what we suppose to be god may not be God at all; what passes for God, even amongst Christians, may not be worthy of the name. There is such a thing as Christian idolatry, and, if Psalm 82 is on the right lines, whether belief in God promotes justice or injustice is an acid test of it.

God the Question

So, we need to start somewhere deeper than 'a supernatural being' and bland generalizations like 'God is the answer to all our questions and problems'. What if, as theologians have suggested, God is not so much 'the answer' to all our questions, but the question itself? And what is 'the question'? Perhaps something like this: 'Why is there something, rather than nothing?' 'How — or why — do we and this extraordinary world come to be here at all?' The question of God and its practical implications — the question this book seeks to address — is arguably the deepest and most important of all.

We should not jump in too readily with answers. At this stage we might simply note the title of a book by a leading theologian of the late twentieth century, Eberhard Jungel, *God as the Mystery of the World*. Perhaps we can also agree that the universe is not self-explanatory, as if it begged no questions at all. Earthquakes may prompt us to ask 'Why?' But so, too — in a very different spirit — might a gloriously sunny morning, or the arrival of a new-born baby.

Christians and atheists need to converse more often. That might help Christians to move beyond the Christian idolatry which is sometimes confused with real belief in God. It might also help atheists to clarify what they are denying. But are we still talking about two diametrically opposed groups of people here? 'Christians believe in God, atheists do not.' I suggest that it is not quite so simple. Just as we can't understand 'atheism' without asking what the atheist is denying, so we won't understand Christian 'theism' without appreciating both what Christian faith affirms and denies when it talks about God.

Early Christian 'Atheists'

The early Christians were accused of being atheists. The second-century *Martyrdom of Polycarp* says that the crowd, 'amazed at the noble conduct of the Godloving and Godfearing race of the Christians, shouted out "Away with the atheists..."' Justin Martyr, also writing in the second century, explains that, like Socrates, 'we are called atheists'.[8]

Christians were accused of atheism in those early days because they did not believe in the gods of the Graeco-Roman world. That might seem to make those second-century accusations irrelevant today. I am not so sure.

On the Benefits of Reticence

The Psalmist's testimony against the atheistic 'fools' of his day sounds intolerant. But, as I suggested earlier, translating a verse directly from its original context to ours is not always wise, because it could easily be misunderstood. As we've seen, for the Psalmist the 'atheist' was a doer of evil. What did he deny? Perhaps, in the Psalmist's view, the God of Israel, who, according to the Old Testament, was the God of justice. To recall Rowan Williams' argument, we need to know what an atheist is denying in order to understand his atheism.

The Old Testament insists unwearyingly that the God of Israel is 'like no other', as Psalm 82 claimed. That may sound like the worst kind of religious arrogance and intolerance. But if — and at this stage in the argument it can only be 'if' — 'the gods' are agents of oppression, humankind is clearly better off without them. The question, then, becomes: can God — the God of Israel (to give God one of his Old Testament titles) — do any better?

What atheists deny may vary. If they deny the existence of 'a supernatural Being', that is not necessarily a denial of the God whom Christians believe in. As theologians down the centuries have taught, God is not 'a being' or even 'a Being', but, in some mysterious sense, 'Being itself'. The so-called 'apophatic' tradition of Christianity has always insisted that it is easier to say what God is not than what God is. It is a healthy caution.

Are answers about God, for the Christian at least, supplied by Jesus? Again, we should not fall back on well-worn Christian clichés. Even the person of Jesus raises searching questions: a man crucified on a cross who, according to two of the four Gospels in the New Testament, died in agony exclaiming that his God had forsaken him (Matthew 27.46; Mark 15.34). The cross raises in a very acute form the issue of religious idolatry.

Christian Idolatry

Are Christians guilty of idolatry? The answer to that is surely 'Yes'. When a person's local church becomes the sole focus of their devotion and commitment, or, worse, when their 'faith' prompts them to send hate-mail to someone they passionately disagree with, then, I believe, they are falling into what I am calling Christian idolatry. Such idolatry takes subtle forms. It might be a person's particular version of Christianity, for which they are prepared to fight tooth and nail. I write this in the week in which the British House of Commons debated same-sex marriage. The media report that MPs on both sides of the argument have received vitriolic mail from religious as well as non-religious people.

When something (or someone) absorbs a person's total devotion, then that something functions as their 'god'. (I return to the subject of contemporary 'gods' in the Conclusion.) Such idolatry, even when it is Christian idolatry, always makes a person less human. For one thing, he — or she — cannot be the friend of someone who is the enemy of their idol; idolatry is always divisive. Some honest self-examination, not least for religious people, helps: '…in prayer…the risk of falsehood and idolatry is evident: we run the risk of creating for ourselves a God in our own image and likeness, and making prayer an act of self-justification and self-reassurance in which we remain closed within ourselves'.[9]

So, like 'atheism', the meaning of the word 'theism' is not as obvious as it sounds. For Jew and Christian alike, the Bible has some searching things to say about God and god-substitutes. A preliminary test for everyone might run like this: 'Show me what kind of person you are, and I will tell you what kind of god you believe in'. This brings me to a final point here about Christian belief in God.

Belief in Practice

Most people who profess a Christian faith live, at times, as though God did not exist at all. We are just not consistently Christian; for example, we spend our money or go about our daily work, and our belief in God makes little or no practical difference.

Of course, a quick response comes to mind: 'None of us is perfect; none of us really practises what we preach'. True enough. Yet such a response is too easy. It raises the question of what belief in God really is. If, in answering a questionnaire, a person ticks the box against the words 'Do you believe in God?', does that count as belief? It is easy for anyone, religious and non-religious alike, to be atheist in practice; that is, their belief in God makes little or no difference to the way they live. But the Bible's teaching about belief in God, whilst immensely varied, has one consistent emphasis: belief in God is a very practical affair. Otherwise, it is not really belief in God at all.

4. The God of the Bible

Contemporary Accusations

The atheists to whom I referred earlier are fiercely dismissive of the God of the Bible. Hitchens devotes two whole chapters of God Is Not Great to the Bible. He dismisses both Testaments in successive chapters: 'Revelation: The Nightmare of the "Old" Testament' and 'The "New" Testament Exceeds the Evil of the "Old" One'. As the chapter titles suggest, these are extreme, mostly ill-founded, arguments. To claim, for example, that the Gospels 'cannot agree on anything of importance' is simply inaccurate. Both writers are selective in what they choose from the Bible to discuss. It is a pity that such intelligent writers have not seriously engaged with biblical scholarship. Or if they have, it does not show.

And yet, there is a case to answer. Anger, violence and jealousy in abundance are attributed to God, mainly in the Old Testament. The New Testament, however, has by no means a clean sheet. But, for all its difficulties, the Bible is the key to a way forward. I believe it has the potential to bring about a theological revolution. By that I mean the Bible

has the depth and breadth to transform our understanding of God —
provided we read it with more imagination and self-awareness, and less
literally and dogmatically. Using the Bible as ammunition to try to
discredit opponents is not a good idea. Christians throwing texts at each
other like custard pies are never a pretty sight. Literalist interpretations of
the Bible are likely to discredit both the Bible and God.

All of this will require as much re-thinking from Christians as from
people who do not hold the Christian faith. Christopher Hitchens, in a
chapter called 'Religion Kills', cites many recent and contemporary
examples of how religion has incited or colluded with violence and
terrorism. He notes courageous people who 'protested in the name of
their religion', and who put humanity before religion. He adds, I think a
little unfairly, that their courage was a complement to humanism, not
religion.

Against Hitchens and many others, I hope to show that the Bible is the
foundation for a far-reaching Jewish and Christian humanism. But that
involves recognizing that the Bible is a collection of writings which is
both religious *and anti-religious*. We do not understand the religion it
champions unless we also understand the kind of religion it rejects. And
crucial to both understandings is what the Bible says about God.

Key Questions about the Bible

The range of the Bible is vast. We should expect that from a collection of
sixty-six writings whose origins span the best part of a thousand years.
Can we make any sense at all of this bewildering variety? Biblical
language is a multi-layered kaleidoscope, comprising imaginative poetry,
rhetoric, narrative and teaching in which it is difficult to separate out
historical fact and theological interpretation. Does it add up to a coherent

picture of God? At first sight, it seems not. On the one hand, God orders the massacre of other nations (e.g. Deuteronomy 7.2); yet the writer of 1 John in the New Testament tells us 'God is love' (1 John 4.8, 16). This is only one example of the Bible's contrasts and contradictions.

In writing this book, I have tried to keep three questions in mind:

1 How consistent are the Bible's many portrayals of God?

2 Can the Old and New Testament understandings of God be reconciled? Marcion, of the second century CE, thought not, but that has never been the majority Christian view. But the idea that the New Testament 'fulfils' the Old is not as straightforward as it sounds either.

3 Should we recognize that the Bible is uneven in quality, especially in what it says about God, and allow some sections a bigger say than others? If so, how do we decide that? We can't entirely exclude our own preferences from how we interpret the Bible. On the other hand, our interpretation can't be just a 'pick and choose' exercise; it has to consist of far more than our personal preferences.

Conclusion

We need to read the Bible well. By that I mean: how can we read the books of the Bible in ways which do justice to their character and purpose? So, here is a working definition of the Bible's authority: concentrate on the Bible's *effects* on us, its readers. Its purpose is

- to enable human life to become what human life is meant to be,

- to enlighten humans with a truth which is liberating,

- to promote personal and communal growth in faith, hope and love.[10]

If the Bible does these things, its readers can agree to differ about a great deal else.

* * *

Three Questions for Reflection and Discussion

1   'Taken for granted', 'a problem', 'a question': do any of these words describe your own views about God?

2   How much, if at all, does our understanding of God come from the Bible? Is the Bible as much a hindrance as a help?

3   Is it enough to 'mothball' discussions of the Bible's authority and inspiration, and concentrate instead on its effects?

Going Deeper: Further Reading

A.E. Harvey, *Is Scripture Still Holy?* (Eerdmans, 2012).

K. Ward, *Is Religion Irrational?* (Lion, 2011).

Endnotes

1   An entry found on the last page of the diary of the poet Edward Thomas after he was killed in World War One in France, April 1917.

2   *Children's Letters to God*, compiled by Eric Marshall and Stuart Hample (Fontana, 1976).

3   J. Taylor, *The Christ-Like God* (SCM, 1992), p.1.

4   C.S. Rodd, *The Book of Job* (Epworth, 1990), p.127.

5   R. Dawkins, *The God Delusion* (Bantam, 2006), p.31.

6   R. Williams, *Faith in the Public Square* (Bloomsbury, 2012), p.281.

7   K. Armstrong, *A History of God* (Vintage, 1999); quotations from p.5.

8   Quotations from *A New Eusebius*, edited by J. Stevenson (SPCK, 1957), pp.19 and 62.

9   E. Bianchi, *Words of Spirituality* (SPCK, 2002), p.58.

10 On reading the Bible well, see also my 'Seven Steps' below.

Seven Steps towards Reading the Bible Well

Some ways of reading the Bible are better than others, but the Bible itself doesn't provide a D-I-Y kit for that purpose. So, sit lightly to theories about biblical authority and inspiration, without necessarily rejecting them. I make this suggestion, not because I don't believe in them — I do — but because there is a better test of whether we are reading the Bible well than the theories with which we sit down to read it. That test is a simple one: what kind of person is the Bible making me?

With that in mind, here are some suggestions:

1   Read the Bible with an open mind and heart, attending to its words as you would to a conversation partner.

2   Remember that all its verses have their own context:
   - a literary context: the passages before or after the one you are reading will usually shed some light on it.
   - a social and cultural context: the biblical past for many of us today is like another country; look out for different, even strange ways of saying and doing things.
   - historical contexts:
     - what was going on in the writers' world at the time they wrote,
     - the words you are now reading?

3   Read imaginatively — without letting your imagination run riot.

4   Be prepared to revise your views as you listen to your 'conversa-
    tion partner' if you are beginning to notice things you hadn't
    noticed before, and to realize the Bible doesn't say what you
    thought it said.

5   If you read it as a Christian, consciously make the person of Jesus
    Christ the 'lens' through which you interpret the Bible. At the
    same time, don't let the voice of the New Testament drown the
    voice of the Old.

6   Read the Bible with others when you can — or read the insights
    of other people in books you can trust — e.g. a good Bible com-
    mentary. (But note that commentaries vary in quality.)

7   Be committed or open to the Bible's underlying purpose: love —
    for God and neighbour.

Some readers may be unhappy that there are no explicit references here
to prayer and the Holy Spirit. I ask you to re-read these 'steps', and to
consider that both, though not explicitly mentioned, are strongly implied.

As for 'God', as you read,

- be prepared to revise your understanding of God,
- don't jump to conclusions on the basis of one or two
  passages,
- remember that the 'God' referred to in the text can't
  always be straightforwardly equated with the real God.

1

God of Beginnings

'Almost everything in the Bible is about creation'

For readers who are Christians and for readers who are not, Genesis, the first book of the Bible, is full of surprises — or it ought to be. What is the reader to make of the God portrayed here? God speaks when there is no one to speak to, and asks questions as though he[1] didn't know the answer. God also punishes people when today many would say 'Give them a second chance'. God even, on one occasion, destroys everything and everyone, except for a select band herded into an ark to escape a flood. After the world has dried out and normal life resumes, God knocks down the first skyscraper. And this is just the first eleven chapters.

The Bible ought to be a culture shock. Unfortunately, some of us have read it (or misread it) so often, we no longer know what it really says. Readers who are new to it might well wonder 'Who on earth is God?', given this mixed bag of stories (if that's what they are). But it seems reasonable to begin at the beginning.

In this chapter we shall:

- explore the creation stories of the Bible's first book, Genesis, particularly in the light of modern science and the theory of evolution,

- question the traditional Christian understanding of 'the Fall' and suggest a more biblical understanding of human freedom and maturity,

- look critically at stories in Genesis about God's destructiveness, and

- anticipate (as Genesis does) the unfolding story of God and humankind.

1. In the Beginning, God

Evolution and Creation

The young teacher being interviewed was clearly desperate to get the job. Asked whether he would teach creationism or evolution, he replied, 'I can teach it either way'. We may sympathize with his caution; the debate between evolutionists and creationists is often sharp and intolerant. Some Christians insist that you can't be a Christian, or at least not a 'Bible-believing' Christian, and believe in evolution at the same time.

This 'either–or' approach over-simplifies both options. Evolution isn't something to believe in as if it were a creed or a dogma. It's more like a working model of the world which allows for more questions. We need to approach the Bible, too, without preconceived ideas about what it's about. We can believe that it conveys to us the word of God without subscribing to a literal interpretation of its first chapter.

Unfortunately, many who do not share the Christian faith suspect that modern science has disproved the first sentence of the Bible (Genesis 1.1) that 'in the beginning' God made the world. It is a tragedy that the argument about what the Bible teaches about creation has become polarized as well as over-simplified. There are faults on both sides.

Fundamentalists damage the credibility of the Bible when they insist that their view of the Bible and its authority is the only correct one. But Richard Dawkins also over-simplifies. Some Christian arguments, as he alleges, are weak: for example, explaining gaps in our knowledge about the universe by recourse to God.[2] But creationism and fundamentalist religion are easy targets, and Dawkins gives the impression that they are the only options on the Christian table.

Christians who are scientists, philosophers or theologians — or a mixture of all three — have pointed out how inadequate and extreme some of Dawkins' arguments are. For one thing, the Bible's teaching about creation is not an explanation of how the world began, even though many Christians think so. The word 'explain' gives the wrong impression, implying that the Christian view and the 'big bang' theory about the universe's origins are in competition with each other.

The Bible's teaching about creation is more profound, varied and challenging. In any case, the opening verses of the Bible are not its only pictures about the origin of the world. There are pictures also of how God 'cleft the sea monster in two' in making the world (Psalm 74.13; compare Psalm 89.10 and Isaiah 51.9-11). We need to recognize when the Bible's language is factual, and when it is imaginative, pictorial and meta-phorical. 'Sea monster' language is clearly pictorial, and to ask whether God slew this sea monster before, during or after the making of the world in seven days is clearly absurd. But rich and varied though the Bible's teaching about creation is, Genesis 1 — obviously — has pride of place.

Most peoples of the world seem to have had their stories and myths about the creation of the world. (I have a little book of African creation myths on my shelves.) The Hebrew people were not alone in fashioning their stories about creation; most peoples of the ancient world did so, and themes from other creation myths of the ancient Middle East, such as Babylon's, are woven into the story here. Should this surprise us — or trouble us? Not at all, especially as the biblical picture is distinctive in all kinds of ways. For example, there is nothing nationalistic or tribal about the first chapter of the Bible.

The picture of creation in Genesis 1 is both distinctive and profound. Take the Hebrew word *bara*, meaning 'create'. It is only ever used of God; it begins and ends the first story of creation in the Bible (Genesis 1.1; 2.3). So, whatever is meant by 'create', it is something God does — and only God. The Bible insists again and again that God made heaven and earth and everything in them (e.g. Psalm 146.6; Acts 17.24).

Something Out of Nothing?

Humans, of course, create and make, but usually we make things out of something else — for example, a table out of existing pieces of wood. But God did not make the universe — with all its countless galaxies — out of something; God made it out of *nothing*.

Dorothy Sayers' book *The Mind of the Maker* explores this crucial point well. We can't literally make something out of nothing, but God does. Sayers compares God making the world with someone writing a play, referring to the idea of a Russian theologian, Nikolai Berdyaev, that

God created the world by imagination. A letter from former Archbishop of Canterbury, Rowan Williams, to a six-year-old girl who wanted to know how God was 'invented' expresses this with an engaging simplicity. The little girl's enquiry was couched in the form of a letter to God; the archbishop's reply is expressed as if it were God's:

Dear Lulu,

Nobody invented me — but lots of people discovered me and were quite surprised. They discovered me when they looked round at the world and thought it was really beautiful or really mysterious and wondered where it came from... There was nothing and nobody around before me to invent me. Rather like somebody who writes a story in a book, I started making up the story of the world and eventually invented human beings like you who could ask me awkward questions![3]

A writer or a composer is the best analogy for God the creator. Creation is a work of God's imagination: creation out of nothing. But Jews and Christians believe that the world itself is not imaginary; God really has given it — and us — life: creation out of nothing. St Paul puts it like this:

God...gives life to the dead, and calls into existence the things that do not exist (Romans 4.17).

So, creation is a mystery. The Bible itself begins rather mysteriously:

'In the beginning when God created the heavens and the earth, the earth was a formless void and darkness covered the face of the deep, while a wind [or spirit — the same word in Hebrew] from God swept over the face of the waters.

The original words are a bit ambiguous. There may be a footnote in your Bible giving a different translation: 'When God *began to create* the heavens and the earth...' A later verse says God finished the job (Genesis 2.1), probably meaning the job of bringing order out of chaos. Elsewhere the Bible seems to say that this was only the start. Jesus in John's Gospel says of God:

> My Father is still working, and I also am working (John 5.17).

God's sustaining and nurturing of creation continues, even though God's initial 'creation' is done.

So, the Bible begins very grandly. Yet we can't imagine a time before the beginning; scientists can't observe it. We can't analyze or dissect the claim 'God created'. But we can ask, in the light of the whole Bible, what it *means*.

The Mystery of the World

A basic 'rule of thumb' in interpreting the Bible is this: 'every text has a context'. That is true of the Bible's very first chapter, whose context is, quite simply, the rest of Genesis. So, the role of this creation story — Genesis 1.1–2.4 — is to witness, not so much *how* God creates and creatures came to be, but rather, as a number of scholars have pointed out, how God *blesses* his creation. If that is correct — and I believe it is — it's not difficult to show that the whole of the Bible is about creation: God's purpose for it and his intended blessing of it.

Christians often try to explain too much. The doctrine of creation doesn't explain *how* the world began; it announces a mystery. The claim that God 'made' the world does not contradict the 'big bang' theory or other theories offered by contemporary science. The comment of the science correspondent of a leading British newspaper is worth noting:

> Physics has compiled a convincing history of the universe, except for the first second or so. But we cannot explain why the universe is as it is or even why it happened at all. Biology and palaeontology have outlined a convincing chronicle of life's development and colonisation, but the opening chapters are obscure and the beginning a mystery. Primate evolution is an exciting story with missing chapters, but we have no real idea why one species can ask abstract questions, compose poems and write books about the history of the universe.[4]

It's tempting for religious people to try to fill in the gaps by reference to God. But that's a mistake. In a similar way, to call God the 'first cause' is to introduce a scientific term where it doesn't belong. 'Creation' language doesn't — or need not — contradict science. To talk about 'creation' is to talk about God, and about faith, meaning and purpose. Explaining things, identifying cause and effect — that's the domain of science. But, as with Christians and atheists (see the Introduction), there is a lot to be said for theologians and scientists talking to each other.

The Order of Creation

So, 'creation' in the Bible is about much more than beginnings, as its very first chapter tells us. It portrays in majestic language a universe of order and rhythm. Everything has its place: light is separated from darkness (v.4), the 'water under the heavens' is gathered into one place (v.9), there is the rhythm of day and night (vv.4-5, 8 etc), and so on. The question is not the science but the meaning. The young Dietrich Bonhoeffer, theologian and Lutheran pastor executed by the Nazis in 1945, wrote these words about the rhythm of day and night long before our 24/7 societies:

> ...for us the creatureliness and miraculousness of the day has completely disappeared... We no longer allow ourselves to be determined by the day. We count and compute it, we do not allow the day to give to us. Thus we do not live it. Today less than ever — for technology is a campaign against the day.[5]

Of course, many people have to work nights; otherwise, our way of life, with its immensely complex inter-dependence, would begin to unravel. But there is a far deeper question here about limits: limits to growth, consumption, power. We have our place, and according to the Bible, God has given human beings a very exalted place. But it still has its limits.

What the Bible says about the order of creation isn't limited to its opening chapter. This theme runs through the Old Testament and on into the New. Old Testament writers and editors saw correspondences between the creation of the world and the building of God's temple in Jerusalem. It was as if the whole world was God's sanctuary, and the temple itself was an entire world, as a Psalmist recognized:

> He built his sanctuary high as the mountains,
> Founded like the earth to last for ever (Psalm 78.69 REB).

Another psalm brings together the wonders of the heavens and the joy of God's law (Psalm 19.1-11).

So, the theme of creation in the Bible spreads far and wide, and that should not surprise us. It embraces God's temple and its worship, God's law and the way of wisdom. Nothing is left out — except, perhaps, darkness, and the waters of chaos. But more of this shortly.

2. Human Beings and God

A Good World and Its Shadow

There is another prominent detail in this opening chapter of the Bible. The writer repeatedly says that what God is making is good (vv.4, 10, 12, 18, 21, and 25), with a final, grand affirmation:

God saw all that he had made, and it was very good (v.31).

This is not so easy for us to affirm, familiar as we are with 'nature red in tooth and claw'. The people of the Bible were familiar with that, too. Yet for us the extraordinary advances in photographic technology mean that we can now watch on TV the world of nature in a way that no previous generations were able to do. For myself, I find television nature programmes often inspirational, though the way in which one species preys on another may make it more difficult to sing the old hymn with its line, '"Yes God is good", all nature says'. Yet, as theologian Keith Ward has argued, there is also a lot of cooperation in the world of nature, and even 'selfish genes' co-operate and sacrifice themselves.[6]

The Psalms of the Old Testament insist that all creation praises its Creator. For us humans, it's not usually so simple. We sometimes find it hard to join in this chorus of praise, and to see what, according to

Genesis, God saw — namely, that creation is good. To us it often looks much more ambiguous.

There are no easy answers. The ultimate answer, in the view of the Bible, lies in the character and purpose of God. God is good, and that is why the same may be said — eventually — of God's creation. In the meantime, there are two problems: the problems of evil and of suffering.

Christian faith has traditionally maintained that the world in the beginning was perfect. But then came 'man's first disobedience' and 'the Fall' (the stories in Genesis 3 and 4). Yet even before the Fall, there are hints that maintaining the goodness of his world is not going to be all plain sailing for God. What is 'darkness' doing here (Genesis 1.2-5)? Is it benign — i.e. just the opposite of day ('...the darkness he called Night')?

There is an *aetiological* purpose behind some of these stories in Genesis; that is, they aim to *explain* things, such as why night follows day. (*Aetia* is the Greek word for 'cause'.) But they go deeper, as well. So, is the darkness more than just the opposite of the day? Certainly, later in the Bible, it is — as in John's Gospel: 'The light shines in the darkness, and the darkness did not overcome it' (John 1.5). The final light, when there will be no more night (Revelation 21.25), only comes at the very end.

For now, darkness remains, as do the waters of chaos. For now, God has put them in their place (Genesis 1.6-9; Psalm 104.5-9), but biblical writers know full well that humankind colludes with anti-creation forces. (On this, see especially Jeremiah 4.23-28 and Revelation 11.18.) Their final defeat awaits the end (Revelation 21.1).

Before we leave this first creation story, we note its climax.

God's Day of Rest

> So God blessed the seventh day and hallowed it, because on it God
> rested from all the work that he had done in creation (Genesis 2.3).

Sunday observance is a much-neglected theme in our day. Sunday, of
course, in biblical terms, is the first day of the week, the day of Christ's
resurrection (Mark 16.1); it is not the 'sabbath' — i.e. the seventh day.
British Christians, however, spent much of the twentieth century
escaping the long shadow of Victorian 'sabbatarianism', a negative,
moralistic attitude to Sunday. To caricature for a moment, 'Thou shalt
not enjoy thyself...'

Yet the 'sabbath' — to keep for the moment the Old Testament and
Jewish term — is a central part of the Bible's teaching about creation.
Genesis 2.1-4 represents only the beginning. Later passages, such as
Exodus 23.9-12, show how the Sabbath became an institution for the
benefit of the needy.

So, here is another example of how 'the doctrine of creation' (to give
this theme its 'official' title) is about far more than the universe's origins.
A 'sabbath' is an integral part of creation's well-being. But what was, or is,
God's 'rest'? Did God down tools in the way that any of us might do at
the end of a working day? The words we use about God are never so
simple — which is just as well, or God would simply be one of us writ
large. Whatever it means, God clearly hasn't finished whatever God is
doing (John 5.17, 'My Father is still working...'). But whenever God
finishes, God invites humankind to share his rest:

> ...a sabbath rest still remains for the people of God (Hebrews 4.9).

Or will there be a foretaste of that rest even before the end? The New Testament suggests as much.

Two Creation Stories, Not One

'Every text has a context'. For Genesis 1, that means the whole of Genesis — but also, and more immediately, another creation story (Genesis 2.4–3.24). Here is a second 'account' of creation: the story of Adam, Eve and the Garden of Eden. Both accounts cannot be literally true, and the editors of Genesis must have realized that. So, the question to ask is: how do these two creation stories complement and interpret each other? Two examples must suffice.

First, the two stories give different pictures of God. In Genesis 1, God is 'centre-stage', directing operations from start to finish: a transcendent, almighty God. In Genesis 2, Adam, Eve and their 'world' are more centre stage, and here God is portrayed in a much more human way: God near at hand. The two pictures complement each other.

Second, Genesis 1 and 2 give complementary pictures of human beings. There is a 'higher' view — made 'in God's image' (1.27) — and there is also a 'lower' view — formed 'from the dust of the ground' (2.7). What 'made in God's image' means is far from clear, and there have been many suggestions. But it may mean that humankind is called to be God's representative; God appoints the human race as 'God's royal stand-in'. If so, this is an extraordinary sharing of responsibility. It doesn't make humankind co-creators with God, but it does make creation open-ended, not closed.

God's image might also mean our capacity as human beings to relate to God, to each other and to creation. But we're still made from the dust of the ground' (Genesis 2.7); as we recognize now, we have evolved from the animal world. In these 'high' and 'low' views there is both glory and challenge.

The role of humans as God's 'stand-in' helps to show what human 'dominion' over all other creatures (v.28) means. Despite the violence attributed to God in the Bible (on this, see Chapters 2 and 3), God takes pleasure in the world he has made (Psalm 104.31). Amongst the many things God does, he notices when sparrows fall (Matthew 10.29), and he clothes wild flowers with glory (e.g. Luke 12.27-28). So, God's dominion is not exploitative or oppressive in the way that human dominion has been. Imitating God — e.g. God's holiness (Leviticus 11.44-45), love and forgiveness (Ephesians 4.31–5.2) — is a recurring theme in the Bible.

According to the Bible's first two chapters, the question 'Who is God?' is bound up with questions about human beings. The Creator God seems bent on partnership with the human race. How that will work out will be one of the Bible's main themes. For now, we note that the first creation story portrays human beings made for God, the second — with a much more 'human' God — gives a picture of God as Adam's friend.

3. The Question of God's Patience

Fall from Grace

The narrative moves on. Humans were to 'fill the earth and subdue it' (1.28). Their expulsion from Eden (3.24) is the first step towards that. So, Adam and Eve's disobedience, it seems — like human ambition in the story of the Tower of Babel (11.1-9) — serves God's purposes. Staying put in one place and building sky-ward was not what human beings were supposed to do; they were to 'fill the earth' by spreading outwards, not upwards.

The second creation story of Adam and Eve in the Garden of Eden, prepares the way for the story of 'the Fall' which follows. Unfortunately, Christian thought about the Fall has often been as muddled and wrong as it has been about creation. We imagine that this story tells of how God gave humans the freedom to choose, we chose wrongly, and that was the fall.

This is a misleading 'take' on several counts. God begins to look like a teenager's parents reluctantly giving him the front door key for the first time. So here, God gives the two occupants of Eden the opportunity to taste 'the forbidden fruit', though not without a dire warning (Genesis 2.16-17). This line of thought tends to fuel contemporary atheism. It suggests that the first step to maturity is to rebel against the parent god who infantilises us and prevents us from growing up.

Many have just such a concept of God. But whatever Jesus meant by becoming 'like children' (e.g. Mark 10.15), it can't mean that God would rather we stay as the naive children Adam and Eve were in Eden. Yet this ancient story is still a story about us, our freedom and maturity. We need to see what the Bible says about these things, if we are to make sense of the God of the Bible.

When Will the Human Race Come of Age?

It might be asked: what sort of freedom does anyone have if they're forever shackled to their Creator? But God's freedom does not threaten human freedom; according to the Bible, God is the way to it. Marriage at its best is a key to understanding this. It's true that some think 'marriage ties you down'. However, if a marriage is the marriage of equals, whose love for each other grows and deepens as time goes by, that is not what happens. Of course, each partner is likely to make sacrifices for the other, but their relationship is both their joy and, therefore, their freedom.

People have to grow up before they can marry, and 'growing up' is crucial to understanding the first three chapters of the Bible. Christian tradition has long celebrated what, in previous centuries, the Church called Adam's *felix culpa* — literally, his 'blessed blame': if Adam hadn't sinned, Christ would not have come. To put it another way, if Adam and Eve (*alias* the human race) are to mature, they need to leave the garden.

If we understand human history in the light of evolution, as we surely must now, the truth behind the Adam and Eve story still stands: human beings need to mature: to become what God intended us to be. But the coming of Jesus has to be re-thought a little. Christ's coming becomes, not an emergency measure in response to Adam's sin, but rather the turning-point and goal of creation.

In the light of evolution, of course, we can't say when humans reached the point where we could be described as 'sinful' in a way that animals are not. But 'sin' is a word necessary to understanding what the Bible says both about God and human beings. 'Sin' means that our God-given capacity for relationships — with God and with each other — does not work as well as the Creator intended, and so none of us has fully grown up. (On the important biblical word 'sin' see also Chapter 6.)

Our Freedom and God's

God is free simply to be himself, and in his freedom God has created a world and humans in God's image. And just as God's freedom isn't a threat to ours — that would be an immature view of God — so human freedom isn't a threat to God's freedom either. In fact, the myth of the Fall, set in the context of the whole Bible, especially St Paul's teaching, is about humans losing our God-given freedom by losing our 'original' relationship with God — i.e. what God intended. On this understanding, we are only ever truly free when we are as God intended us to be.

The Enlightenment and modern thought has skewed our thinking about this ancient story of the Fall. We tend to have a very individualist, secular view of human freedom: freedom from restrictions, freedom to exercise our rights, freedom to choose. It's a one-sided, secular view of freedom, aided and abetted by a consumerist society. In the biblical view, our freedom lies ahead of us — in a maturing relationship with God.

So, in all kinds of ways, the first three stories in the Bible set the scene for all that follows. This first beginning 'introduces' a God who made a universe which he pronounces 'good', and who makes human beings in his own image to look after it all. In order to do that, we need to grow up, and that involves re-discovering the friendship of God which we took for granted in our own innocent beginnings in Eden.

God's 'Destructiveness'

From Genesis 3.23, human beings find themselves out in the big wide world, the Garden of Eden left behind. From this point on in the Bible we begin to encounter God's apparent destructiveness. I say 'apparent' because we cannot attribute to the real God — i.e. God as God really is — all the words and actions the Bible attributes to God. This by no means demolishes the Bible's authority — rather the opposite. So, we call the stories of Noah and the Flood and the Tower of Babel (Genesis 6.9–8.22 and 11.1-9) 'myths'; they didn't happen, but they are still stories which convey truth about God and humankind.

God's destructiveness in the Bible has not surprisingly been the cause of fierce criticism. Richard Dawkins, surprisingly for an Oxford professor, complains that deciding which bits of the Bible 'to write off as symbols or allegories' is a matter of 'personal decision' by theologians.[7] In fact, it's not so much personal decision and preference as using intelligence and common sense in deciding what kind of literature it is you're reading. There is room for disagreement, but distinguishing fact from fiction, prose from poetry, history from myth in the Bible is not as arbitrary as Dawkins appears to think.

Once we have abandoned a literal interpretation, which does justice neither to the facts of history nor to God, we begin to see what the myth of the Flood might mean. Human beings, entrusted with looking after God's world, drive their Creator to despair:

> Now the earth was corrupt in God's sight…and God said to Noah 'I have determined to make an end of all flesh, for the earth is filled with violence because of them…' (Genesis 6.11, 13).

And yet, in spite of this, God, by the end of this story, has a change of heart and resolves to 'stick with' his creative project:

...the Lord said in his heart, 'I will never again curse the ground because of humankind, for the inclination of the human heart is evil from youth; nor will I ever again destroy every living creature as I have done' (Genesis 8.21).

It's as if God has now recognized what he has taken on in creating human beings. If God hadn't realized this before, he certainly has now. 'It is God who has changed, not humankind... In this verse the entire relationship between God and his creation has shifted. God's very graciousness now means he forsakes his absolute power.'[8]

God's covenant with Noah and his descendants — i.e. the entire human race (Genesis 9.8-11) — sets the seal on this new relationship between God and humankind. This is the first of many covenants between God and humans in the Bible. In this one God commits himself not just to humans, but 'to every living creature' — a sobering thought in our day, when humankind is threatening the survival of more and more of our fellow-creatures.

The rainbow which God then puts in the sky (9.13-17) is a sign of the covenant. Of course, we now have a scientific explanation of how rainbows appear. That makes the Genesis aetiology (why things are as they are) redundant. But the deeper meaning behind the story still invites our consideration: God's commitment to his world. That is something which, as we shall see, the Bible invites us to believe in for other reasons.

These opening chapters of Genesis contain another example of divine destructiveness: the story of the Tower of Babel (11.1-9). This story, unlike the earlier stories about Cain and Noah, has no note of divine grace to soften the severity of the divine sentence. But what follows is a new beginning which, in effect, reverses that sentence. A later story — of a multi-lingual but harmonious community (Acts 2–11) — is the climax. For now, God now begins all over again.

4. Beginning Again: Abraham, 'Friend of God'

God's Covenant and Promise

How does God begin again? In a nutshell, God chooses Abraham. Why Abraham? The Bible doesn't say. It gives no character references for Abraham. He could have been anyone. And perhaps that is the point. God invests a great deal in Abraham — everything, perhaps. Later tradition called Abraham 'the friend of God' (e.g. James 2.23). God calls him (Genesis 12.1-9), and makes a solemn covenant with him (Genesis 15 and 17).

Embedded in every covenant God makes with humans there is always a promise. God made a promise to Noah after the Flood ('Never again...', 9.11). To Abraham God promises a new country and a great future (12.1-2; 15.7; 17.8), a son (15.6; 17.16); he will be 'the father of many nations' (17.4). These themes, God's covenant and God's promise, are themes which, like two closely intertwined golden threads, will run and run right through the Bible.

At this point, we must face head-on a historical question: does it matter if Abraham, Isaac and Jacob never existed? I'm tempted to say: it had better not. There are not many scholars today who would say that they did, and even fewer who would argue for the historical accuracy of the stories about them. But the focus of the Bible (and of the book you are now reading) is the reality of God, and we should not make the reality of God dependent on the historical reality of Abraham.

To return to Genesis 12.1-9, God's promise to Abraham was deeply un-promising. God promised to make his 'kindred' a 'great nation', but Abraham was already 75 years old and had no son. God ordered him to 'the land that I will show you' (v.1), but the land was already occupied' (v.6), and yet God insists, against all the evidence to the contrary, that the land will be Abraham's (v.7). God in the Bible seems to go in for these un-promising promises, as one story about Abraham powerfully shows.

Two Dark Stories about God

Abraham's behaviour, in the chapters which follow, has been strongly criticized, and understandably so. To pass off his beautiful young wife, Sarai, as his sister in order to save his own skin (Genesis 12.10-20) is hardly the conduct of an officer and a gentleman. (By chapter 20 Abraham still hasn't mended his ways.) But the focus of Genesis is the promise of God, not the character of Abraham. So how will God keep his word to Abraham, with all these odds stacked against him?

Two further stories about Abraham are especially difficult for us in the way they portray God. First, God informs Abraham of his intention to destroy the cities of Sodom and Gomorrah for their wickedness (18.16-21). Abraham's bold mediation on their behalf — the first instance in the Bible of someone accusing God of injustice[9] — brings about a stay of execution (18.22-33), but only a stay (19.28-29); Lot, as Abraham's nephew, escapes just in time (19.15-23). The second story is that of God commanding Abraham to offer his son Isaac as a sacrifice (Genesis 22.1-19).

What are we to say about the character of God here? First, we are not dealing with history. We should not think that God really said and did all that these stories attribute to him. But can they still teach us anything about God? They can't if they are taken literally and out of context. So, the story of Sodom and Gomorrah should never be cited as an example of how God hates 'practising homosexuals'. (On this subject, see also Chapter 6.) As for the story of Abraham and Isaac, we need to look at that more closely.

Every Text has a Context

Most of us have been influenced in the post-enlightenment era, whether we realize it or not, by the German philosopher, Immanuel Kant. Kant argued that if, as in this story, God seems to command someone to do something which is against the moral law, then that command cannot possibly come from God. But this natural response to the story misses two important points. First, the religious background out of which this story grew strictly forbade child sacrifice and, second, the context of the story is God's promise to Abraham. So Abraham is not just any old human being, but, in the Bible's view, the bearer of human destiny in the mysterious purposes of God. In the Bible's unfolding story, the Creator has started all over again with his call to Abraham.

So, is God just playing games here? If this story were true, we might say so. Instead, in Jewish tradition, this story becomes 'a paradigm for the Jews' commitment to God's will…'[10] God is not the monster he would be if this story were literally true, but, even so, people can still feel that God is asking the impossible of them, as Jesus appears to have done (e.g. Mark 14.36).

From a later Christian perspective, words of St Paul give a different slant to this ancient story: God 'did not withhold his own son' (Romans 8.32). Eventually — or should we say, from the very beginning? — God is revealed as self-sacrificial. But that is not obvious. 'Wrestling' with God is part of the journey (Genesis 32.22-32; Luke 22.44), and, in the biblical story, it's still early days.

'Coat of Many Colours'

The last fourteen chapters of Genesis tell the story of Joseph, popularized in the modern musical, *Joseph and the Amazing Technicolor Dreamcoat.* In these chapters God takes a back seat most of the time. But when references to God do occur, they make clear that God is shaping events to fulfil his purpose (e.g. 39.21, 23; 41.16, 52; 45.5-9; 46.1-2). Genesis ends with a scene of reconciliation between Joseph and his brothers after the death of their father, Jacob. Joseph forgives his brothers and expresses the narrator's conviction that, throughout, God has been working out his purpose:

> Even though you intended to do harm to me, God intended it for good… (50.20).

But we can't simply leave the matter there. The Bible's stories prompt many questions: how does God 'work' in the world, 'answer' prayer, give people guidance? These stories come from long ago; the context, the culture, the language are so different from ours, and we can't read off simplistic, literal answers to questions like these. (We shouldn't assume *they* did, either.) But people who believe in God and attribute a special authority to the Bible will still draw an over-arching story (a meta-narrative) from these narratives: God's creative project is on its way. The outgoing God has committed himself to his world and to the descendants of Abraham. That is what 'covenant' means in the Bible.

5. Summary

The first book of the Bible introduces us to the story of God and the story of humankind. God creates a whole world, including human beings who reflect God's own capacity for creativity, relationships and promise-making. The two creation stories focus on origin, meaning and purpose; their truth deepens and illumines the explorations of science.

The story of the human 'fall' is not about our freedom to choose, but our unfulfilled potential for partnership with God and the freedom and maturity which goes with that.

God's destructiveness in Genesis should not be understood literally. Its sequel — God's covenant with the human race, symbolized by the rainbow, and God's call of Abraham — suggest that God doesn't give up easily in the face of human shortcomings. In fact, God's covenant and promise will run like golden threads right through the Bible.

6. Looking Ahead

For Christians, the themes of God's promise and covenant run on into the New Testament and reach a climax there. Several writers claim that all things were created 'in' Christ (Colossians 1.16) or 'through' him (Hebrews 1.2; compare John 1.1-5). The theme of creation figures in the New Testament as well as the Old. So, there is much to be said for thinking of the coming of Jesus as evolution's pivotal point and goal: self-sacrifice, co-operation and community are at the heart of all things, even more than selfish genes and the survival of the fittest.

So much in the Bible is inter-connected: creation, the sabbath, the Law of Moses, the Temple in Jerusalem and — this, especially, for the Christian interpreter — 'Adam' (the Hebrew word for 'human') and Christ. Adam is 'the first human', Christ 'the last' or ultimate human (1 Corinthians 15.45). Paul compares and contrasts Jesus and Adam in Romans 5.12-20, and declares that God's 'new creation' is what finally matters (2 Corinthians 5.17; Galatians 6.15; compare Revelation 21 and 22). We might think almost everything in the Bible is about creation, and we would probably be right.

In the end, believing in creation is not really a theory about how the universe began. It is, first, a reflection about a mystery: why is there something rather than nothing? It is, second, wonder and awe at just what there is, and, third, gratitude: in the words of the old hymn, 'Glad that I live am I'.

* * *

Three Questions for Reflection and Discussion

1   'The whole of the Bible, not just the opening chapters of Genesis, is about creation'. Do you think this is an exaggeration?

2   'To think that science and belief in God are incompatible is to misunderstand both'. Do you agree?

3   Does the approach to the Bible suggested thus far make the Bible easier to understand? Does it enhance or threaten our ideas about the Bible's authority?

Going Deeper: Further Reading

Claire Amos, *The Book of Genesis* (Epworth/SCM, 2004).

Nicholas Lash, *Believing Three Ways in One God* (SCM, 1992, 2002).

Jon D. Leveson, *Inheriting Abraham: The Legacy of the Patriarch in Judaism, Christianity and Islam* (Princeton University Press, 2012).

Endnotes

1   Personal pronouns referring to God can't be entirely avoided without stylistic or linguistic contortions. 'He', of course, doesn't mean that God is male. All our language about God is approximate; it can hardly be otherwise.

2   R. Dawkins, *The God Delusion* (Bantam, 2006), pp.125-28.

3   Printed in *The Daily Telegraph*, 25 April, 2011.

4   Tim Radford, reviewing *The Universe Within: A Scientific Adventure* by Neil Shubin (Allen Lane, 2013) in *The Guardian* 2 February, 2013.

5   *Creation and Fall* (SCM, 1966, though first written in 1932–33, and published in 1937), p.26. Bonhoeffer's insightful little book has informed this chapter at other points.

6   K. Ward, *Is Religion Irrational?* (Lion, 2011), p.54.

7   Dawkins, *The God Delusion*, p.238.

8   Clare Amos, *Genesis* (Epworth, 2004), p.53.

9   Jon D. Leveson, *Inheriting Abraham: The Legacy of the Patriarch in Judaism, Christianity and Islam* (Princeton University Press, 2012), p.63.

10   Leveson, *Inheriting Abraham*, p.112.

2

Moses, Joshua
and the Violence of God

*God — the real God — did not do and say everything the
Bible says that he said and did.*[1]

We need to read the Bible more imaginatively than many of us were
taught to do. We need to develop an ear for its different kinds of
language: fact and fiction, prose and poetry, literal statements and
metaphorical ones. It will not do to wheel out lazy arguments like 'Where
do you stop?' or 'Isn't this the thin end of the wedge?' If indeed there is a
Creator, might not that Creator expect us to use our brains, rather than
read the Bible in a literal, wooden way?

There is an important consequence of reading the Bible more
imaginatively: it is, as I suggested in the last chapter, to recognize that
God — the real God — did not say and do everything the Bible says that
he said and did. This is a further, important step towards reading the
Bible well, and towards understanding what it really teaches about God.
For now, let me recap on themes from Chapter 1.

The Bible tells the story of God and humankind. But to say it is a 'story' does not mean it is fiction. If there is truth in the Bible, this truth lies deeper than both fact and fiction. To summarize the story thus far: from 'the beginning', God gave humankind a privileged place in his creative project. Made in God's image, invited to share in God's gentle rule over creation — the real meaning of 'dominion' — Adam and Eve (*alias* the human race) start off as innocent children in their parent's garden. It can't stay like that, and it doesn't. According to the story, God's creative project goes badly off course.

God could have given up, but doesn't. The sign of the rainbow at the end of the story of the Flood means God will do whatever it takes, and his call to Abraham marks a new beginning. But now we must turn our attention to other books of the Bible and some of their major themes.

In this chapter we shall:

- examine the stories of Israel's 'Exodus' from Egypt and her conquest of Canaan,

- explore some biblical language which, if taken literally, becomes a shocking example of divine brutality,

- consider the underlying theological theme: God's protective 'jealousy' towards Israel.

There is much to engage us, to put it mildly, about the portrayal of God here.

1. God the Terrorist?

Over many years I have heard religious people express severe views about individuals or groups on whom the Bible is also severe: idolaters, homosexuals, 'the Jews' (as in John's Gospel), Judas... It's quite a long list. Some Christians say we should 'love the sinner, but hate the sin'. But I suggest that (a) this often-quoted view misrepresents God, and (b) it's impossible, in practice, to make that distinction anyway.

We need to face some uncomfortable facts about the Bible. 'The Bible has a dark side that is not often acknowledged by those who regard these texts as Scripture.'[2] The author of these words, Eric Seibert, goes on to ask 'What does the Bible do to you?' There is a related question: what understanding of God are we working with here? A God who, then — and now? — favours some nations over others? A God who used the hapless Judas to fulfil his purposes? A God who sacrificed the peoples of Egypt and Canaan in the interests of his favourite, the people of Israel?

The Story of the Exodus: Fact or Fiction?

'The Exodus' is the story of how God rescued the Hebrew people from slavery in Egypt. First, God inflicted on Pharaoh and the people of Egypt a series of plagues, culminating in the deaths of their first-born sons (Exodus 7–12). Then, as Pharaoh and his army pursued the escaping Hebrews, God miraculously parted the waters of the Red Sea for them to make their getaway, allowing the returning waters to engulf and drown the Egyptians (Exodus 14).

There are many allusions to this story in the Bible. Most Christians assume it happened because it's in the Bible. But what if that assumption is wrong? What if this is a mistaken understanding of the Bible's authority?

There is in fact no historical evidence for the exodus from Egypt or the plagues with which the story says God punished the Egyptians. 'We are a long way from history here; no disaster of this kind is known from any independent source…'[3] Other commentators make a similar point. But they also say: that is not the point of the story.

So what was the point? The story of the Exodus from Egypt was invested with enormous significance. Together with God's call to Abraham, Isaac and Jacob, it becomes the foundation story of Israel. What is more, it reveals what God is like: One who is concerned for oppressed people such as slaves. As with the story of Abraham, I want to suggest that this claim about God's character does not depend on the historical truth of the story.

Some may say, 'If it's in the Bible, isn't that evidence enough?' But, to repeat the point made in the first chapter, we should not make the fundamental category mistake of gauging the authority of the Bible by its historical accuracy.

Protestant Christians, in particular, need to extricate themselves from the mental (and, perhaps, spiritual) straitjacket in which they often find themselves when thinking about the Bible. Why should a story narrated in the past tense be history, rather than fiction? Why couldn't an inspired writer have imaginatively elaborated a story — with or without an historical nucleus? Truth — the truth which makes us free — is bigger than a string of historical facts.

God the Sadist?

The real problem with this story is not so much historical as theological. Are we really to suppose that God inflicted all those terrible plagues on the people of Egypt? We rarely address awkward questions like these. We give biblical stories like this one a positive title: 'the Exodus', or 'the Liberation of the Hebrew Slaves', rather than 'The Sufferings of the People of Egypt at the Hands of God'.[4]

I'm not sure we Christians have grasped this nettle yet. We accept biblical stories too readily at face value. But did God really unleash a series of plagues on Pharaoh and the Egyptians because they tried to stop God leading his people out of Egypt? The traditional answer has been: this is what happens to enemies of God, to people who oppose God's will and purpose. That, I suggest, is an impossible view for seriously religious people — Jew, Muslim, and Christian alike — to hold today.

Quite apart from what this says about the character of God, consider the moral consequences. At the climax of the story, with the Egyptians reeling from the dreadful climax of the plagues, the deaths of their first-born, the narrator tells us that they were simply fair game for whatever looting the Israelites chose to engage in:

> The Israelites…asked the Egyptians for jewellery of silver and gold, and for clothing, and the Lord had given the people favour in the sight of the Egyptians, so that they let them have what they asked. And so they plundered the Egyptians (Exodus 12.35-36).

No amount of special pleading can excuse the implied morality of this story. The fact that the story-teller has twice told us already (Exodus 3.19-22 and 11.2-3) that this is what will happen doesn't lessen the theological and moral problem. The theological and moral go together: if God can torture and kill the Egyptians, why shouldn't his people help themselves to whatever was going?

I hardly need add that religious wars down the centuries have been 'justified' by reference to biblical stories like these.

God and the Red Sea

The story gets worse. The waters of the Red Sea, miraculously parted to enable the Hebrew slaves to escape, returned and swamped the pursuing Egyptian army — and all of this the work of God (Exodus 14.28-30).

Yet not everyone accepted this story without a qualm. There was a later rabbinic tradition in which God forbade the angels to sing a song of praise for the destruction of the Egyptians: 'The work of my hands has been drowned in the sea, and you want to sing songs?'[5] The Exodus raises a question hugely relevant for our day: if God exists, does God ever champion one nation against another? We shall need to return to this question.

Still an Iconic Story

Many people, especially the victims of slavery in modern times, have believed that the God who liberated the Hebrews slaves is the champion of oppressed people always and everywhere. There is much in the Bible to support that view; it does not depend on the Exodus being an historical fact. Can we still find the same iconic power in a story which now turns out to be fiction not fact? I believe we can, and, for good theological reasons, we must. Genocide is always an offence against humanity, so how can a credible God possibly engage in it?

Behind the story of the Exodus there may be ancient folk memories of the liberation of oppressed slaves. It was a truly formative story; its influence runs through Old and New Testament alike. (See, for example, Isaiah 43.2 and 44.27.) It was a nation-shaping, faith-shaping story. It reminded the people of Israel of the kind of God they believed in: champion of the oppressed and scourge of tyrants; liberator of slaves and judge of their oppressors. Such a story does not have to be historical in order to be iconic and — in the most profound sense — true.

What also matters is the effect stories like this have on their hearers and readers. So, the questions 'Does God engage in violence?' and 'Does God have enemies?' are inescapable and urgently relevant.

We turn in a moment to another famous story in the Bible. But before we do, it may be helpful to indicate, however briefly, how the books of Exodus, Leviticus, Numbers and Deuteronomy relate to the overall understanding of God in the Bible.

'Thou shalt not'

A small number of passages are well-known to Christians, as well as to Jews. The Ten Commandments (Exodus 20.1-17), with the repeated 'You shall not' (Commandments 6–10) have helped to create a negative view of God, and a parody of John 1.1: 'In the beginning was the word, and the word was "No"'. More positively, as a distinguished scholar once observed, they set an important biblical pattern: what God requires follows on from what God has done for his people. ('I am the Lord God who brought you up out of the land of Egypt', v.2.)

Christians influenced by St Paul's writings and perhaps their own tradition are inclined to dismiss much of this section of the Bible as 'legalistic'. That would be unfair and inaccurate. The author of Psalm 119 repeatedly says what a joy and a delight the law of God is to him (vv.16, 35, 70). God's law is an integral part of the universe (v.89), the way of wisdom. Like God's Temple, it belongs to the order of creation. There is more to be said, especially in the light of the teaching of Jesus and of St Paul. (On this, see Chapters 5 and 6.)

2. 'Divine' Massacres, Ancient and Modern

Joshua and the Battle of Jericho

Richard Dawkins does not spare the book of Joshua: 'a text remarkable for the bloodthirsty massacres it records and the xenophobic relish with which it does so'.[6] His militant atheism should not obscure the challenge here for Christians. Whether it happened or not, says Dawkins, isn't the main issue. He's quite right about that. The biggest problem is that, in the story, God ordered the massacre of the Canaanites: divinely sanctioned genocide. (See the summaries in Joshua 10.40 and 11.16-20.)

Dawkins makes three complaints. First, many Christians appear to pick and choose which passages in the Bible they understand literally and which they interpret symbolically. But by what criterion do they decide? That is a fair point, though, as I have already suggested, using their common sense and intelligence is a good start. Second, some Christians still take the Bible literally, and the results are sometimes toxic. It's difficult to argue with that.

Thirdly, says Dawkins, most religious people, including Christians, don't get their morality entirely from the Bible anyway. That is partly true, and should cause no surprise. The Bible itself is eclectic: a section of Proverbs in the Old Testament is very like Egyptian proverbs of the time, and Paul borrows some of his moral teaching from the culture of his day. So, Christians don't — and can't — base all their moral conduct on the Bible alone.

Modern Massacres and the Bible

Clearly, when the Bible appears to sanction genocide, we need to monitor its effect on its hearers and readers. The story of the conquest of Canaan in the book of Joshua has been iconic in modern history — to the great cost of the indigenous peoples of America, Australia and New Zealand. An American Indian, Robert Allen Warrior, states the problem with passion and cogency. In a chapter tellingly entitled 'A Native American Perspective: Canaanites, Cowboys and Indians', Warrior notes how natural it was for the white settlers to identify the 'Native Americans' with the Canaanites; after all, they were the people who already lived 'in the promised land'. He recognizes that the actual history may have been different from the stories narrated in the book of Joshua, but that doesn't solve the problem:

> No matter what we do, the Conquest narratives will remain. As long as people believe in the Yahweh (Jehovah) of deliverance, the world will not be safe from Yahweh the conqueror.[7]

Just so. However uncertain or even improbable these narratives are as historical accounts, the theological problem remains: they are testimonies to the violence of God. Along with the story of the Exodus, the Conquest story is a major example of God vindicating one nation — God's nation — at the expense of others. No amount of special pleading — God did it reluctantly, see how the story 'ends' in the New Testament etc. — mitigates the problem of verses like this one:

> So Joshua defeated the whole land…he left no one remaining, but utterly destroyed all that breathed, as the Lord God of Israel commanded (Joshua 10.40).

God's Violence in the Bible

Most of Joshua chapters 6 to 11 are, or should be, difficult for the person who is troubled by the apparent violence of God. It might be argued that this genocide never happened, and that seems to be true. There is no archaeological evidence which proves conclusively that it did, and given the violence and destruction described here, we would expect such evidence if it had happened. As with the Exodus, this is a story which has been filtered through the memories and experiences of the people of Israel over many centuries; it would have been told, re-told and edited many times.

But, as with the Exodus, the theological and ethical problem remains, even if the Conquest never happened:

> Those who try to justify the Canaanite genocide…do so because of their preconceived idea of what the Bible says and does… They must find some way to explain God's behavior and to defend God against charges of wrongdoing.[8]

How is it that we have reached the twenty-first century without seriously addressing this fundamental theological and ethical problem? It has been creeping up on the Church for some time, but most Christians either look the other way, concentrate on 'nicer' bits of the Bible, or offer arguments which totally fail to justify the picture of God given in Joshua — i.e. God ordered the genocide reluctantly. (The lectionary widely used in the churches today tends towards a sanitized or censored version of Scripture.) If the outrage of atheists like Richard Dawkins and Christopher Hitchens, and the post-colonial protests of writers such as Robert Allen Warrior have finally forced this problem on our attention, well and good.

To recap, the book of Joshua cannot be read as if it were straight-forwardly historical. But even so, we are still left with (a) the problem of a God who commands genocide, and (b) the moral implication that believers in that God can therefore do the same. (Christian and Western imperial history offer all too many examples.)

3. Divine Cruelty to Dumb Animals?

The Conquest stories, like the story of the Exodus, should be seen as a story of liberation. It is a story about the giving of land to the landless — for that is what the Israelites were. But what of the poor Canaanites? Presumably they were God's children, as the Egyptians were. We need to look more closely at the details, rather than see them as the hapless victims of a divine juggernaut.

Kings — a Good Thing or a Bad Thing?

Canaanite kings feature in the book of Joshua, and kings in the Bible often, though not always, spell trouble. Only God is king, so human kings are impostors or tyrants — perhaps both. Biblical writers were in (at least) two minds about Israel's kings. They were, in the first place, a grudging concession on God's part, and a source of endless trouble (e.g. 1 Samuel 8). Other nations had kings (v.4) — another reason why Israel should not.

But the Bible also has positive things to say about a king, and especially about 'the house of David' (e.g. 2 Samuel 7.11b-16; Psalm 73; Luke 1.69). There is, however, an odd, but important characteristic of bad kings in the Old Testament which will help us in our interpretation of the book of Joshua: you can tell who a bad king is because, like as not, he will have 'horses and chariots'.

The prohibitions of Deuteronomy 17.14-17 are revealing: don't appoint a king 'as all the surrounding nations do', and — a second prohibition consequent upon the first — your leader 'must not acquire numerous horses, or send men to Egypt to obtain more horses' (v.17). A sure sign that Absalom was on a slippery downward slope was providing himself with a chariot and horses (2 Samuel 15.1). True, Solomon doesn't appear to fit the pattern (1 Kings 4.26; 10.26-29), but not long after this, even he goes the way of most royal flesh — at least, royal flesh with such accoutrements.

Horses, Chariots and God

Readers might be wondering what this equine detour has to do with God. The answer is that 'horses and chariots' in the Old Testament is a loaded term. A verse in a psalm succinctly expresses Israel's *credo* on the matter:

> Some boast of chariots and some of horses,
>
> But our boast is the name of the Lord our God (Psalm 20.7;
> compare Psalms 33.16-19; 76.6; 147.10).

Israel's 'chariots and horses' were of a very different kind, as the death of Elijah (2 Kings 2.11) and a story about Elisha (2 Kings 6.15-17) show. Elijah's own title says it all: 'the chariots and the horsemen of Israel' (2 Kings 2.12). In other words, the stories attached to these two prophets bear similar testimony to Psalm 20: the real strength of Israel was her God and the prophets of God. St Paul's repeated adaptation and quotation of a verse from Jeremiah makes a similar point:

> Let the person who will boast, boast in the Lord (1 Corinthians 1.31;
> 2 Corinthians 10.17; compare Jeremiah 9.22-23).

All of this goes to show why a verse in Joshua which is so repellent to the modern reader should not be read as an example of divine cruelty to dumb animals:

> the Lord said to Joshua, '...Hamstring their horses and burn their
> chariots' (Joshua 11.6, 9).

First, the real God said no such thing and, second, 'horses and chariots', as I have tried to show, is a loaded expression in the Old Testament. To put it another way, this language is not historical, but *ideological*. 'Horses and chariots' are what oppressive kings and dictators have; by the standards of the time, weapons of mass destruction.

If Richard Dawkins protests at what might seem to him a cavalierly 'symbolic' interpretation, there is a simple response:

1   note carefully the words of the Bible *and their contexts*,

2   use your intelligence and your imagination and

3   interpret the Old Testament in the light of the New. (I shall return to this point later.)

The Moral Challenge of the Book of Joshua

Modern history has badly skewed our reading of the book of Joshua. Christians shooting from the hip and carrying all before them in the Americas, Africa and Oceania may well have drawn inspiration — mistakenly and tragically — from these texts. The painful results of their often arrogant conquests are still with us. And it is deeply ironic that many Christians who today object to the violence of the book of Joshua have supported wars waged in their name in Iraq and Afghanistan. Joshua is better seen, not so much as the story of a conquest as a story of liberation: land for the landless in the face of oppressive monarchies.

It is worth adding that the book of Judges, immediately after the book of Joshua, gives a significantly different picture: 'So the Israelites lived among the Canaanites...' (Judges 3.5). Even the book of Joshua recognizes that there were exceptions to the massacres (Joshua 11.19).

Admittedly, to recognize that the Conquest never happened and that some of the language of the Old Testament here — about kings, horses and chariots — is ideological, not literal, still leaves us with our basic problem: God is portrayed as commanding genocide. We cannot say it too often: God cannot have said and done all that the Old Testament portrays God as saying and doing. The real God is very different.

A moral evaluation of the Conquest story, like that of the Exodus, is a challenge that Christians today must face. It was quite normal for a nation to portray its god as a divine warrior in the ancient world, and in this Israel was no exception. But this is by no means all that the Bible, Old and New Testaments alike, has to say about God. Today we have begun to reject militant-sounding hymns such as 'Onward, Christian soldiers' (though we still have a long way to go). We must similarly critique the Bible. We cannot go on ignoring or trying to justify texts which attribute cruel behaviour to God.

Some may wonder what will be left if we critique the Bible in this way. My answer is: a very great deal. The Bible remains the unique, indispensable 'classic' for Christians. But its role in moral formation is crucial: does it help its readers to keep more fully the two key commandments to love God and our neighbour?

4. A Jealous God?

The two stories of the Exodus and the Conquest are especially important for us to look at as we try to see what kind of God the books of the Bible speak of. We can't remind ourselves too often that there is much in the Bible that we mustn't take at face value; not everything narrated in the past tense is factual history. But we still need to look at a fundamental theological theme behind these stories and many other passages in the

Bible. This is the theme of 'election': God's choice of Israel — the corollary of God's covenants with Abraham, Moses and the people of Israel. Many passages give expression to it, such as,

> ...you are a people holy to the Lord your God; the Lord your God has chosen you out of all the peoples on earth to be his people... (Deuteronomy 7.6-8).

God's Love Affair with Israel

The idea of God choosing one nation or particular people in preference to others is a difficult one. But, as we are seeing, this language of 'election' is frequent — even fundamental — in the Bible. It helps, I believe, to link the idea of 'election' with the sense of vocation and responsibility. For example, a person might feel a particular 'lure' towards a particular job or career, even thinking, if the lure is strong, that that is what they are 'meant' to do — their 'destiny', even. In a similar way, two people who fall in love might say that they were 'meant' for each other.

In the Bible, however, there is one especially difficult feature. God chose Israel, and is portrayed again and again as championing them *at the expense of other nations* — notably, as we have seen, in the stories of the Exodus and the Conquest. But there are other difficult, unappealing features of the Old Testament, such as its references to God's 'jealousy'.

Admittedly, God is not portrayed as saying 'I am a jealous God' very often — only six times in fact, including the two versions of the Ten Commandments in Exodus and Deuteronomy (Exodus 20.5; Deuteronomy 5.9). But the *theme* of God's jealousy is much more common. And that is a problem — or at least it should be.

Many texts express or imply the jealousy of God — the books of Exodus and Deuteronomy, the stories of Israel's past in the books which follow, as well as the prophets. What are readers of the twenty-first century to make of this unattractive quality which the Old Testament attributes to God? We can't get round the difficulty by saying that the word 'jealous' crops up in only the Authorized Version. It's there in the NRSV, the REB and the NIV as well, whilst the GNB translates Exodus 20.5 by 'I tolerate no rivals', words which we are likely to associate with the world's worst dictators. So what is God jealous about?

God and Other Gods

Mostly, God's 'problem' is other gods. Five of the explicit references to God's jealousy occur in the contexts of warnings about other gods, whilst the sixth (Nahum 1.2) has a reference to God's enemies. So, when the Bible says 'jealous', it means it — or so it appears.

'Sexual jealousy', however, doesn't sound quite right, even though the Bible often uses sexual imagery in this context. Unlike the gods of ancient Greece and Rome and the gods of other ancient mythologies, Israel's God is, according to the Old Testament, 'like no other'. In particular, this God doesn't engage in sexual intercourse with either goddesses or human females. But if we ask ourselves who, according to the Bible, *is* God's partner, we shall be taking the first step towards understanding what all this 'jealousy' is about.

God does not engage in sex but God does have a human partner. From the beginning God engages with the human race. That is a remarkable phenomenon in the theologies of the ancient world. God is more a 'people' than a 'places' God — more 'God of Abraham' than (e.g.) 'God of

Bethel', even though God in the Bible is sometimes associated with certain places — particularly Jerusalem. And, as we saw in the last chapter, one of the key words in the Bible for God's engagement with humans is the word 'covenant'.

Covenants and Marriages

God's covenants with human partners are many: the covenant with Noah and the whole of creation (Genesis 9.10-17), with Abraham (e.g. Genesis 15.18), with Isaac and Jacob (e.g. Genesis 28.13), Joseph and his descendants (Genesis 50.23), with the whole nation of Israel (e.g. Exodus 34.10), with David and his descendants (2 Samuel 7.11-16); in due course, there is the promise of a new covenant (e.g. Jeremiah 31.31-34).

This covenant, constantly renewed, is the basic reason why God is *jealous for Israel*: God has called them, out of all the nations of the earth, to serve and to worship him as a 'kingdom of priests', God's 'holy nation' (Exodus 19.5-6).

The Old Testament often uses family imagery — father and son, husband and wife — to express the two-way relationship of this covenant. Hosea is one of several Old Testament prophets to deploy the image of a marriage. On the one hand, God commits himself to Israel; Israel may depend upon the divine faithfulness, and God, in turn, expects Israel's faithfulness and obedience. So, because God loves Israel, God is 'jealous' when Israel is unfaithful. (Deuteronomy 7.7-8 and 10.15 are two passages which tell the story of God's love for Israel.)

God the Husband

Some of this marital imagery is, frankly, offensive. Old Testament scholar Walter Brueggemann observes how God is always cast as 'the authoritarian husband', and Israel as the 'easily blamed, readily dismissed, vulnerable wife', suggesting both intimacy and violence. Two passages from the prophet Ezekiel (16.32, 38, 42-43 and 23.25-30), focussed on the destruction of Jerusalem, are especially difficult. In a world increasingly, and rightly, conscious of violence in marriage, I do not wish to minimize the unpleasantness of some of this imagery in the Bible. God as a jealous husband is not a pretty sight. What are we to make of it?

First, 'the husband' is the Creator of the world, the personal Reality who imagined the world into existence. So, the 'marriage' between Creator and creatures could hardly be an open one; the Creator can't stop being our Creator. Second, the Creator, by definition, can't have any rivals, even though God in the Bible may sometimes sound jealous of them. But, third, we need to keep in mind what, according to the Bible, those 'rivals' (idols) do to Israel, *alias* the human race.

We come back to these themes shortly. But first there is a more general point to be made about all the language we use about God.

The Way We Speak about God

For centuries Christian tradition (and other faiths) has emphasized that it's easier to say what God is not, than what God is. (On this, see the Introduction, section 3, 'God and gods'.) By contrast, the Old Testament — much more than the New — often uses *anthropomorphic* language of God, such as God's 'arm' or God's 'face' — that is, a human image applied to God which cannot be literally true. So, difficult as the 'jealousy' language is for us, it's still worth asking: when the Bible calls God 'jealous', what does it mean?

Idols: Reality or Illusion?

The Bible — Old and New Testament alike — is ambiguous about whether idols are real. They are not real — and yet they are. Psalm 115 (vv.4-8) is one of many Old Testament passages which scoff at idols: they can't do anything; they are made by humans! St Paul says something very similar (1 Corinthians 8.6). So, idols don't actually exist. And yet their power is very real. Above all, idols distract Israel — and, we might add, the human race — from the Reality the Bible calls 'the Living God'.

To take a modern example, is the power of 'the market' real? A short answer might be: the market has as much power as human beings choose to attribute to it, as Rabbi Jonathan Sacks implies:

> The only thing that makes social or economic trends inevitable is the belief that they are.[9]

But in our day the market is often given a power and quasi-divine status which most certainly distracts human beings from the true God. The same may be said of capitalism — hardly a god, yet sometimes running amok amongst us with destructive power. This brings us to a second key theme in the Bible.

Idols and Humans

I suggest that one reason for God's 'jealousy' or unhappiness at Israel's and our unfaithfulness to him is *what idols do to us*. They make us less than human, they destroy or damage human relationships and human communities. On the one hand, idols are nothing: 'as dumb as a scarecrow in a plot of cucumbers' (Jeremiah 10.5). But this same prophet is aware of the price Israel pays for her idolatries:

> Has a nation changed its gods,
>
> even though they are no gods?
>
> But my people have changed their glory... (Jeremiah 2.11)

St Paul picks up the same theme: idolatry makes us less than human, and our dehumanization destroys relationships and fragments communities (Romans 1.18-32).

In the Bible, idolatry and injustice go together: worship what is less than God, and you will fail to give fellow human beings their due as well. Conversely, the worship of God and what the prophets call 'righteousness' and 'justice' go together. So, we might say that God has good cause to be 'jealous', and this not so much because God has been insulted and offended (even though the Bible's language might sometimes suggest that), but because of the damage God's 'rivals' — i.e. our idols — do to us.

God and the Nations

One consequence of God's jealousy for Israel is that God champions Israel *at the expense of other nations* — most spectacularly in the Exodus from Egypt and in the conquest of Canaan. Many verses in the Old Testament celebrate God's 'victories': for example,

> He showed his people the power of his works,
>
> in giving them the heritage of the nations (Psalm 111.6).

It remains a potent factor in Middle Eastern politics to this day.

The idea that God privileges Israel *at the expense of other nations* has to be re-thought in the light of the New Testament. Later passages in the Old Testament show that re-thinking had already begun — see, for example, Isaiah 55.5 and Zechariah 8.20-23; other passages, however, speak of nations bringing tribute (Isaiah 60). The fundamental theological point is this: we cannot suppose that, with the coming of Christ, the eternal God had a change of heart, or that God inflicted punishment on the Egyptians and Canaanites reluctantly. Rather, the problem has to be grasped: *how are we to understand and interpret the actions which writers of the Old Testament attribute to God?* Biblical language about God cannot be taken at face-value; it has to be interpreted.

So, here are three inter-related themes, if we are to get at what the Bible means by the jealousy of God: God's covenant with Israel; God's horror at what idols do to human beings and human society; and, in the Old Testament though not the New, God's readiness to champion Israel at the expense of other nations.

5. Summary

The stories of the Exodus from Egypt and the Conquest of Canaan are questionable on both historical and theological grounds. It's unlikely they ever happened, and, taken as they stand, they present us with an impossible view of God. The 'God' of the text cannot be straightforwardly identified with the real God.

The phrase 'chariots and horses' in the Old Testament has an ideological function: it symbolises powers hostile to God. It's an example of how we need to distinguish as much as we can the language in the Bible which has to be taken literally, and the language which is more imaginative, metaphorical, or, as in this case, ideological.

The 'jealousy' of God, despite the difficult and sometimes repulsive sexual imagery of the Old Testament, reflects God's commitment to Israel, and, ultimately, God's passionate concern for the well-being of humankind.

The challenge for our interpretation of the Bible is inescapable. The stories we have reviewed here give us a straight choice: either God did what these stories say he did, or he did not; either God engaged in appalling violence, or he did not. The choice amounts to this: we may defend a view of the Bible's authority which assumes that stories like these are historical, or we can try to understand its authority differently.

6. Looking Ahead

Here are more themes which re-surface in a different form in the New Testament. The Exodus became, in Hebrew memory and folklore, the icon of God's 'redemptive' work. God acted as Israel's next-of-kin, rescuing them from slavery in Egypt. As the nation's founding myth, the story became central to their understanding of God. The resurrection of Jesus has a similar importance and function in the New Testament.

The story of the Land is much more difficult. In the New Testament, the Letter to the Hebrews locates the destination of the people of God, like their 'sabbath rest', in heaven, anticipated on earth (Hebrews 4.9-11;

11.10). The early Church's mission to the Gentiles may have meant, for St Paul, that the land of Israel and the city of Jerusalem no longer had a special status in the purposes of God. But that continues to be hotly debated.

As with creation in Chapter 1, we should ask what it means in practice to believe in the God of the Exodus and Covenant. Whilst recognizing the acute limitation of human words for the eternal mystery we call God, I venture to suggest at least this: first, God is for justice and against oppression; it is no accident that most, if not all, major religions, identify compassion as a defining characteristic of God. Second, the covenant (e.g. Exodus 19.5-6; 34.10), like the rainbow in Genesis, expresses God's lasting commitment, in the first place to Israel, and, ultimately (as the covenant with Noah suggests), to the whole of creation. Third, what we really and deeply believe about the character of God slowly but surely defines and shapes our own.

∗ ∗ ∗

Three Questions for Reflection and Discussion

1   What are we to say about the Bible's inspiration and authority if 'the real God' did not say and do what the Bible says he said and did?

2   Is the Bible's language about God's jealousy and its image of marriage applied to God and Israel too offensive and sexist to be helpful today?

3   In reading the Bible in the ways suggested here, are we in danger of re-making God in the image we prefer?

Going Deeper: Further Reading

Richard Coggins, *The Book of Exodus* (Epworth/SCM, 2000).

Eric A. Seibert, *Disturbing Divine Behavior: Troubling Old Testament Images of God* (Fortress, 2009).

Eric A. Seibert, *The Violence of Scripture: Overcoming the Old Testament's Troubling Legacy* (Fortress, 2012).

Endnotes

1   My paraphrase of Eric A. Seibert's distinction between 'the textual God and the actual God' in *The Violence of Scripture: Overcoming the Old Testament's Troubling Legacy* (Fortress, 2012), p.117.

2   Seibert, *The Violence of Scripture*, p.46.

3   Richard Coggins, *The Book of Exodus* (Epworth, 2000), p.61.

4   Seibert, *The Violence of Scripture*, p.42.

5   Coggins, *The Book of Exodus*, p.64.

6   Dawkins, *The God Delusion*, p.247.

7   *Voices From the Margin: Interpreting the Bible in the Third World* (ed. R.S. Sugirtharajah; Orbis/SPCK, 1991, 1995), p.284.

8   Seibert, *The Violence of Scripture*, p.108.

9   Rabbi J. Sacks, *The Dignity of Difference: How to Avoid the Clash of Civilizations* (Continuum, 2002), p.86.

Interlude (1)

Is the Bible Still Trustworthy?

Readers of the Bible used to taking it at face value may be unsure where all this is going. If we start to question whether God really said and did the things which the Bible attributes to God, what solid ground remains? Where will it all end?

The first and most important point is this: God is 'bigger' than the Bible. True, Christians call the Bible 'the word of God', but they often mean different things by that. Some say the Bible *is* the Word, others prefer to say 'the Bible contains the Word of God'. But, whichever view we take, it's still true: God and the Bible can't be identical. The Bible doesn't even call itself 'the Word of God'; that description is reserved for Jesus (John 1.1).

Second, Christians are not a 'people of the book' in the way that Jews and Muslims are.[1] It's better to think of Christianity as 'a religion of a person', as a contributor to a recent book suggests.[2] To put it another way, 'the Bible is not the centre of Christian faith… That position belongs to God, and Christians are called to trust him.'[3]

There is a danger of championing the authority of the Bible at the expense of God. Two verses from the New Testament are often quoted:

'Every scripture [Greek *graphe*, meaning "writing"] is inspired...' (2 Timothy 3.16-17). But 'inspired' doesn't mean 'infallible', and it's doubtful, anyway, whether these verses are referring to the Bible at all, since the Bible as such did not exist when they were first written.

There is another reason why these verses don't 'fit' the Bible. 'Useful for teaching, for reproof, for correction, for training in righteousness...' (v.16) isn't an adequate description of either the Bible's value or its function in the Church. Christian faith claims that its scriptures contain the narrative of a life- and world-transforming revelation. That is far, far more than the claim that they're 'useful for teaching...'

Newer methods in biblical scholarship can help us interpret the Bible. *Narrative criticism* breaks the stranglehold of more history-based methods of interpretation, helping us to see, for example, that many of the biblical writers wrote with imagination and literary skill. So the historical questions 'Is it accurate? Is it historically true?' are not usually the most important questions to ask, even though they may have their place. Instead, it's sometimes more productive to ask: 'Why does the writer tell his story in the way he does?'

Rhetorical criticism recognizes that much of the Bible's language was intended to have an effect: to change hearts and minds. So, a further question to ask is this: what did the writer want his language *to achieve?* This approach, too, helps us to focus not so much on a book's historical accuracy, but on why it was written, and what it was meant to do. And that brings us to what the Bible as a whole is for: to change those who hear or read it.

As for its authority, I have long found this definition helpful: true 'authority' is the source of life, truth and growth. Each of those words must be given their full (biblical) weight. 'Life' doesn't mean mere existence, but life as it was meant to be lived. 'Truth' is not just, or even mainly, factual or historical truth, but the truth which sets people free. 'Growth' doesn't refer to numerical or physical growth, but to becoming the kind of people and communities the Creator intended us to be.

In the light of all this, it's worth asking: what makes a good reader of the Bible?

For Christians, there is an important — though, obviously, not exact — analogy between Jesus Christ and the Bible. Both — in a way not easy to define or explain — are human and divine. But to say of either, 'the more human they are, the less divine they must be', is, from the standpoint of Christian faith, mistaken.

So, is the Bible still trustworthy? Yes, it is — but trustworthy for what? I suggest this: the Bible may still be relied upon to help people find a trustworthy God.

Whatever our questions or convictions about God, we can read the Bible confident that its worth and authority can't be measured by its historical accuracy. The Bible's range and depth, the literary quality of so much of its language, story-telling and poetry, its insights into human nature and its often startling statements about God — all invite the engagement of a reader prepared to converse with this book. And 'converse' doesn't mean either complying unquestioningly with, or rejecting too hastily what your conversation partner — i.e. the Bible — is saying.

* * *

Endnotes

1   J. Barton, *People of the Book? The Authority of the Bible in Christianity* (SPCK, 1988).

2   A more recent book makes a similar point: *The Bible and the Believer: How to Read the Bible Critically and Religiously* (Oxford University Press, 2012), p.85. Its authors, Marc Zvi Brettler, Peter Enns and Daniel J. Harrington SJ, are, respectively, Jewish, Protestant and Roman Catholic scholars.

3   Zvi Brettler, Enns and Harrington, *The Bible and the Believer*, p.160.

3

Through the Darkest Night

From this fiery trial of a nation emerges a deeper awareness
of both divine judgement and of God's forgiveness and love.

In the previous chapters I argued that God cannot have said and done all that the Bible credits him with saying and doing. 'God' in the text is not the same as God in reality. But when we read the Bible differently, what picture of God begins to emerge?

As befits its name and location in the Bible, the book of Genesis sets the scene: in the beginning, God. The creation stories are not 'how', but 'who' and 'why' stories. It's the start of God's outreach to the human race. The stories which follow of 'the Fall' and 'the Flood' reflect the tangled relationship of human beings with their Creator. Yet God's commitment to the world is undiminished.

The call of Abraham, together with the story of the Exodus from Egypt, inaugurates the long history of Israel. This, too, is the story of humankind, as is all that follows. Through all the tortuous twists and turns of the 'family fortunes' after Abraham, the promise of God runs like a golden thread: 'I will bless you'.

But, as we saw in Chapter 2, the blessing of Israel spelt trouble for other nations: for the Egyptians in the Exodus, and for the Canaanites in the conquest of Canaan. I suggested that God's violent activity on behalf of Israel at the expense of other nations should not be interpreted literally; the stories are not historically true. God never has sanctioned genocide, and never will.

In this chapter we shall look at:

- two historical events where, this time, Israel was, in the biblical view, on the receiving end of God's anger: the destruction of Samaria and Jerusalem, the capital cities of the kingdoms of Israel[1] and Judah, respectively, in 721 and 586 BCE,

- the effects of these disasters on Israel's self-understanding and her understanding of God,

- the difficult biblical themes of God's judgements and God's 'wrath'.

Biblical coverage of those two national disasters differs, most of all because the northern tribes of Israel never — as far as we know — returned from exile, whereas some of the Judaean exiles from the southern kingdom did. This Babylonian exile, as it is called, has been aptly described as Israel's darkest night — at least, in the Old Testament period. Other dark nights were to follow — never more so than in recent times.

1. Why Did God Allow This to Happen?

God's Punishment?

These stories are different from many earlier stories in the Bible. We know they happened. The empires of Assyria and Babylon were as real as the later Persian and Roman empires. The traumatic events are narrated in 2 Kings and 2 Chronicles: the deportation of Israel to Assyria in 2 Kings 17.5-23, and the fall of Judah to Babylon, first in 597, and, finally, in 586 (2 Kings 24.13–25.21).[2]

The destruction of Jerusalem and its aftermath were traumatic. The associations of the city with King David and the belief that the Temple was the house of God had led many to believe that it would be impregnable to the assaults of other nations. The extreme anguish — physical and spiritual — caused before, during and after the fall of Jerusalem dominates the books of Jeremiah, Ezekiel and Lamentations. This, and the exile in Babylon which followed, was Israel's 'dark night'.

Why, in the view of Old Testament writers, did God allow these two disasters to happen? The writer of 2 Kings and the prophets of the Old Testament give an uncompromising answer. They were God's punishment of the nations of Israel and Judah for all their wrongdoing. Here is the verdict of 2 Kings on the northern kingdom of Israel:

> Therefore the Lord was very angry with Israel and removed them out of his sight; none was left but the tribe of Judah alone (2 Kings 17.18).

The same sentence is pronounced on the later fate of Judah:

> ...Jerusalem and Judah so angered the Lord that he expelled them
> from his presence (2 Kings 24.20).

In our quest for the biblical answer to our question 'who is God?', what
are we to make of this, and the much fiercer, passionate message of
prophets such as Isaiah, Jeremiah and Ezekiel in the context of these
crises? As far as I am aware, very few scholars have acknowledged that
there is a problem in attributing these terrible events to God, as so many
of the writings of the Old Testament do.

Like the victims of the Exodus and the Conquest — i.e. the Egyptians
and the Canaanites — we airbrush the fall of Jerusalem out of our collec-
tive memory. Much better, we think, to concentrate on the renewal of
hope in exile, as expressed in Isaiah 40–55. Advent is more appealing
than Good Friday. But this story, too, like stories of the Exodus and the
Conquest, is one we must read differently. Even though we are dealing
here with history, and not mere story or legend, the theological difficulty
is the same. We run the risk of obscuring the true character of God by
taking the biblical accounts and explanations at face value.

When an Old Belief No Longer Fitted the Facts

Henry McKeating is one scholar who does not do this. This is what he
has to say about the destruction of Jerusalem by Babylon:

> ...Jeremiah's thesis, and that of his editors, is that Judah's failure on
> the ethical and religious fronts was what ultimately led to disaster
> by provoking divine punishment. Can we conclude that this

interpretation, too, was justified by events? Many readers of the book will doubtless answer unequivocally 'Yes' to this question. But others of us are less satisfied.[3]

McKeating goes on to argue that the prophet's 'thesis' is 'simplistic'. History doesn't seem to substantiate the view that God punishes with disaster nations he disapproves of. And even if God did so, would this lead us to believe in God?

The Old Testament itself reflects the problems we encounter with what McKeating calls a simplistic understanding of history. The writers of 1 and 2 Kings do their best to make the theory fit: a good king prospers, a bad king does not. It doesn't work, although they try. They sometimes point out that it's the next generation which suffers. Solomon, for example, was led astray by 'foreign women', welcoming their gods into his realm (1 Kings 11.1-8). So, God punished Solomon's son, Rehoboam, by taking away from him eleven of the twelve tribes of Israel through the rebellion of Jeroboam. The rebellion had begun in Solomon's reign (1 Kings 11.26-39), but it flared up again under Rehoboam (1 Kings 12.1-20). The writer portrays God as making very clear why this is happening:

I shall do this because Solomon has forsaken me (11.32).

But this 'rule' — good kings prosper, bad kings don't — which the writer seeks to apply whenever he can — simply didn't fit the facts. Later passages in the Bible, including some of the Psalms (e.g. Psalm 73), knew this well.

Two Problem Cases

Kings Manasseh and Josiah were glaring exceptions to the rule. Manasseh 'did what was wrong in the eyes of the Lord' (2 Kings 21.2), yet reigned for fifty-five years; he died peacefully, we are to presume, in his bed (v.17). The later writer of 2 Chronicles *does* make the facts fit the theory, unless he had information the writer of 2 Kings didn't have (2 Chronicles 33.1-20). Manasseh in 2 Chronicles is still wicked — 2 Chronicles 33.9 is almost identical with 2 Kings 21.9 — but his reign in 2 Chronicles ends quite differently: Assyria attacks Judah, Manasseh is imprisoned in (surprisingly) Babylon, turns to God and is restored to his throne. 'Thus', says the Chronicler, 'Manasseh learnt that the Lord was God' (v.13), upon which he instigated a religious reformation (vv.14-17).

The fate of Josiah created the opposite problem: a good king who came to a tragic end. 2 Kings gives him a glowing tribute — better than any king before or since (2 Kings 23.25) — but he was still slaughtered by Pharaoh Necho of Egypt (v.29). The Chronicler, as he did with his account of Manasseh's reign, has a version which fits 'the rule' better. According to 2 Chronicles 35.20-24, the reason why Josiah died was because he ignored a warning from Pharaoh Necho that it was God who had sent him (v.22).

Several books of the Old Testament — e.g. Deuteronomy — work on the premise that good people prosper and live long, and wicked people do not. But it's not difficult to see that the facts didn't always fit the theory; they never have, and they still do not. If this were true, many long-lived dictators of our own day would not have lasted as long as they have. It's a major part of the age-old question: why does God allow these things to happen?

Facing the Facts

Does this mean that we should jettison these books of the Bible? No, but we should read them more honestly and questioningly. Life and history are not so straightforward and simple. Even if they were, there would be still more awkward questions about God to be faced. However, this does not mean that the concept of God's 'judgement' in history is entirely wrong, and we shall return to that shortly.

To return to Israel's suffering at the hands of Babylon — allegedly a divine punishment — how can we make theological sense of it, if the idea that God was punishing them was actually wrong? McKeating suggests:

> The conviction that in the exile Judah was suffering for her sins was an important one at the time. It enabled her people to make sense of what was happening to them. It was a life-saving and morale-saving conviction… Whether a present-day reader should believe it is another matter…[4]

If we reject the belief that the deportation of Israel and of Judah were God's punishment, we face other difficulties. Was this explanation by the prophets a great illusion, fostered by God himself? And if not, then what was it? Addressing these questions will be the subject of the next section.

2. Towards Belief in One God

Disaster and National Heart-Searching

This is a theological problem different from those of the Exodus and Conquest stories, because this time God's own people (by now only

Judah), were themselves on the receiving end of God's wrath — or so they believed. Chapter after chapter in the writings of the prophets, Jeremiah and Ezekiel insist that God brought this disaster on the people because of their sins. McKeating is one Old Testament scholar who has argued that we should not necessarily accept that explanation of the disaster. But what were/ are the alternatives?

The people of Israel could have concluded that 'Yahweh', Israel's God, had been defeated. Given the territorial associations of most gods of the ancient world — Israel's God included — that would not have been surprising. But that was not their conclusion. So, if their God had not been defeated, what alternative explanation was there? The alternative was for the nation to engage in some serious heart-searching: 'Our God is angry with us — why?'

There are examples in our own day of nations which, as a result of a disaster or defeat in war, have engaged in healthy self-criticism. For a brief moment after 9/11 America seemed as if it would do so. But then its president unleashed a war against terror, and America, accompanied by its allies, located the fault in Islamist extremists. That interpretation obviated the need for Western nations to ask, in the manner of the poet, for the grace to see themselves as other nations, especially Muslim ones, saw them.

It is hardly necessary to say that God did not bring about 9/11. I simply make the point that a crisis or a disaster may prompt an entire nation to engage in some healthy self-criticism. In ancient times, when the success or failure of a nation was naturally attributed to the favour or anger of its god, it was different. In Israel, where its God and God's worship and commandments were supposed to be central to that nation's life, it is not surprising that they interpreted their disaster as the wrath of God.

Abandoned by God?

It is possible, though I think unlikely, that Judah might have escaped her fate if her leaders had played their cards differently, or even if Judah had been more faithful to God. The premature death in battle of King Josiah, as we saw in the previous section, showed that piety was no insurance against a marauding super-power next door. And that was the problem. The kingdoms of Israel and Judah, for most of their history, were tiny compared with the super-powers to the east: first Assyria, then Babylon. They were like Estonia next door to Soviet Russia, or Cuba just across the water from the USA. So, we must continue to exercise our historical imaginations.

The destruction of Jerusalem in 586 led to a half-century of exile for many of the inhabitants of Jerusalem. It was a dark time; in the Old Testament period it was Israel's 'dark night of the soul':

> By the rivers of Babylon —
>
> there we sat down and there we wept
>
> when we remembered Zion (Psalm 137.1).

Scholars have increasingly come to see that this 'dark night' was — as some of the questions in the prophetic writings imply — a time of anguished soul-searching:

> Why do you say, O Jacob,
>
> and speak O Israel,
>
> 'My way is hidden from the Lord,
>
> and my right is disregarded by my God?' (Isaiah 40.27).

'Why?' was *the* theological question in this major crisis. It is the Old Testament equivalent of Jesus' cry of dereliction from the cross (Matthew 27.46; Mark 15.34). A crucified nation, like a crucified man, could not deflect the suffering by retaliating. And so the exile in Babylon and its aftermath became a time of national soul-searching, of theological ferment, and — eventually — of creative story-telling and writing. A chastened people reflected, as never before, on their past, their present and their future.]

The Only God There Is

Chapters 40 to 55 of the book of Isaiah are one of the most striking results of this 'dark night'. Most scholars attribute these chapters to a 'Second' Isaiah, an anonymous prophet who preached a message of hope and restoration to the despairing exiles in Babylon. His soaring vision of God constitutes perhaps the clearest expressions of belief found in the Old Testament that there is, in fact, only one God:

> The Lord is the everlasting God,
> The Creator of the ends of the earth (Isaiah 40.28).

Later comes this extraordinary passage: the declaration by the God of Israel that he has called and anointed a pagan ruler, Cyrus of Persia, to be his agent in history:

> Thus says the Lord to his anointed, to Cyrus,
> whose right hand I have grasped
> to subdue nations before him…

I call you by your name,

I surname you, though you do not know me.

I am the Lord, and there is no other;

besides me there is no god.

I arm you, though you do not know me...

I am the Lord, and there is no other.

I form light and create darkness,

I make weal and create woe;

I the Lord do all these things (Isaiah 45.1, 6b, 7).

So out of the dark night of exile came a deeper, refined belief in God. God had not punished his people (though that is what they believed). Instead, God worked in hearts and minds through their torment and anguish.

The theological anguish and the national soul-searching went together. What was Judah really about — what was she *for*? What was her core identity? Could the answer to both questions possibly be — God? There are analogies in our personal experience and in the history of nations. An illness, a crisis, a disaster prompts the question 'Why?' And out of the questioning may come a new resolve, a deeper self-understanding, with purpose and values in life re-assessed.

The Nations of the World

Both Jewish and Christian scholars warn against regarding ancient Israel as xenophobic and exclusivist. Some passages in the Old Testament give that impression, but others do not. These probably come from the period after the exile in Babylon, and so this is probably the place briefly to acknowledge them.

Despite the many prophecies against foreign nations (part of a prophet's 'job spec'), there are exceptions. A remarkable passage in Isaiah (19.18-25) ends with the following divine blessing:

> Blessed be Egypt my people, and Assyria the work of my hands, and Israel my heritage (v.25).

Another passage from Isaiah (56.1-8) expresses a generous hospitality to 'foreigners' and 'eunuchs'; for example,

> Do not let the foreigner joined to the Lord say 'The Lord will surely separate me from his people' (v.3a).

The prophet ('Third Isaiah') goes on to utter words picked up in one Gospel's version of Jesus in the Temple:

> ...my house shall be called a house of prayer for all people (v.7c; see also Mark 11.17).

A third example of wider horizons is the phrase 'coasts and islands'. It's a phrase which occurs often in the book of Isaiah, and especially 'Second Isaiah' (chapters 40–55). It probably refers to 'the Mediterranean in general', and the vision the mission of Israel to 'the non-Jewish world'.[5]

So there are signs, especially in those parts of the Old Testament written during or after the exile in Babylon, of a deepened awareness of that wider world beyond Israel.

Understanding the 'Judgement' of God

My argument thus far might seem to be: the outcome justified the means. But, of course, we cannot justify the destruction of Jerusalem as an action of God on the grounds that it deepened Israel's faith. Imagine a well-meaning person from the local church trying a similar argument with a cancer patient: 'Perhaps God sent the illness in order to strengthen your faith'. It would be pastorally inept, and theologically wrong.

Are we to say, then, that Jeremiah and Ezekiel simply got it wrong? They said 'God is going to punish you' whereas God intended no such thing? In trying to understand their message, we can hardly over-emphasize the pain and suffering out of which it came. Their own suffering, and that of their people, was extreme, and extreme pain is likely to produce extreme language. But central to their message was the reality of God. Ezekiel offers the most God-centred message of all, with his recurring refrain 'I am the Lord'.

So, was their message about the judgement of God simply their own interpretation with no basis in reality at all? The crisis was real, and the theological interpretation of it was theirs. But instead of seeing this national disaster as one inflicted by God as a punishment — as the prophets *in extremis* naturally did, we should understand God's judgement as a 'sifting' process, working through the crises of history, sifting truth from illusion:

> …Divine judgement is not vindictive but purposeful…it dismantles the nation's inadequate categories to make possible new and profound expressions of faith.[6]

So, both the Bible and our own observations of the world suggest that creation and destruction can be two sides of the same coin. History, or at least some of it, might suggest the same. If we were to try to explain the fall of the apartheid regime in South Africa, we should attribute it in large measure to the remarkable life and character of Nelson Mandela. Yet, as I am arguing throughout this book, human input doesn't necessarily reduce divine input. Mandela, one might say, was the leading human agent, God the ultimate agent in the destruction of the apartheid system. Some might wish to make a similar theological claim about the downfall of the Soviet Empire in 1989, although such a claim could never justify the Western triumphalism which we have sometimes witnessed since then.

3. The 'Judgements' of God in History

Making Sense of a Difficult Idea

I put the word 'judgements' here in quotation marks, not because it's a questionable idea, but because it's a difficult, easily misunderstood one. We need to be very cautious in making statements about God at work in history. Wisdom and discernment are needed, and the Bible suggests that only a very small number of people whom it calls 'prophets' have those gifts. However, a 'deist' view of God — a detached or semi-detached being uninvolved in the world — is not compatible with biblical teaching. God is the One 'in whom we live and move and have our being' (Acts 17.28), and God is, as someone once put it, 'a power that makes for righteousness'. A distinguished historian of the last century, Herbert Butterfield, published at least two books on the subject of Christianity and history. In one of them he has this to say:

> ...much though I shrink from the idea of judgment in history, I always have to come round to the view that it does exist.[7]

Thinking of God as an all-powerful supernatural being who controls all that goes on in his world is not helpful here. It is a mistake to think of God as determining historical events in advance, as if God were some great puppet-master in the sky. What if the real God operates more unobtrusively, providing (for example) even the crises and traumas of history with grace, hope and the light of truth? The prophecies of 'Second Isaiah' (Isaiah 40–55) seem to be an example of this process at work in Israel's exile in Babylon.

What is the downside of this? What happens when God's provision of grace, hope and truth doesn't, as it were, get through? To put our question in the language of Dietrich Bonhoeffer, the Lutheran pastor and theologian executed by the Nazis, what happens when God gets edged out of the world on to a cross?' Then, I suggest, we see what the Bible describes as God's 'wrath': a spiritual and moral 'darkness' envelops human affairs. (On this, see the next section.)

Judgement and Love

God did not *bring about* the destruction of Jerusalem in 586 BCE. Rather, God was at work in this crisis, infusing the situation with reason, grace, truth and hope. No situation falls outside this providential power, not even Israel's darkest night in Old Testament times.

The books of Jeremiah and Ezekiel, in their final canonical form, include prophecies of restoration and renewal. Whether they go back to the prophets themselves need not concern us here. (Most, if not all the prophetic writings of the Old Testament, are, in their present form, the result of later editing.) But these writings, including repeated calls to repentance even after the trauma of 586 and exile, remind Israel that the nation needs a new heart (e.g. Ezekiel 18.31) and, amazingly, God will supply it (Ezekiel 36.26-27; see also Jeremiah 31.31-34).

So, from this fiery trial of a nation emerge a deeper awareness of both divine judgement and of God's forgiveness and love. (See especially Isaiah 54.8-10.) As an Old Testament scholar, writing about the messages of Amos and Hosea, reminds us:

> There remains...in the New Testament and in Christian theology, a tension between God's judgement and his love. To lose sight of either is to impoverish the gospel.[8]

What Does God Actually Do?

Before we leave this question, it's important to see the difference in perspective between the biblical writers and ourselves. In this book we are distinguishing between 'the textual God' and 'the actual God'. But our problem with the textual God is made worse by the fact that, to put it crudely, in the Bible God does everything. We don't see things like that — indeed, we might wonder whether God does anything at all. But that difference might be due not just to our scientific knowledge, but also our spiritual short-sightedness.

With that important caveat, we still need to note an important difference between ourselves and the peoples of the Bible, and it is this: they had no concept of secondary causation. So, if the king of Assyria destroyed Samaria, God did it. If Nebuchadnezzar destroyed Jerusalem, God did that, too.

'Secondary causation' may not be the most helpful way to think of our problem. If the creative power of God pulsates or 'rolls' (the poet Wordsworth's word) through everything, we have to ask how God exercises this power. Is it possible that the main sphere of God's action is human hearts and minds, but action in ways which do not undermine human autonomy and freedom? Cooperation with God is perhaps the fundamental human vocation. In an earlier chapter (Chapter 1, section 3, 'The Question of God's Patience'), I suggested that more freedom for humans does not mean less freedom for God — and *vice versa*. God and humans are not competing for the same space.

We cannot prove or disprove the notion that God pre-determines what happens. But we have to live as if God does not. Whatever happens, good or bad, our response matters; we cannot off-load our responsibilities on to God. So, for Israel, in the dark catastrophe of Jerusalem's destruction and the dire suffering of an entire nation, the question was: would this disaster destroy or deepen their faith in God?

It might be wondered whether there were not more important questions: for example, the social and economic recovery of the country after the devastation wrought by the Babylonian armies. That also mattered. But in Israel faith in God and economic recovery went hand in hand.

4. Wrath: God's Dark Side — or Ours?

In the 1980s David Jenkins was consecrated as Bishop of Durham in York Minster. He had already gained some notoriety — partly due to theologically ill-informed newspaper comment — by what he had said about the virgin birth and the resurrection. So when, the day before his consecration, lightning struck York Minster, it was perhaps not surprising that one newspaper led the next day with the headline 'Wrath of God'.

Most people rightly reject such a crude concept of God's wrath. It has, in fact, more in common with pagan ideas about divine anger than with the more profound teaching of the Bible. Yet many stories in the Bible, as we have seen, show that we cannot simply shrug these questions off. Richard Dawkins is one contemporary writer who, quoting fundamentalist evangelists such as Pat Robertson, appears to take a very literal interpretation of passages like these. As with earlier themes about the violence of God, we need to ask how we are to understand what the Bible calls 'the wrath of God'.

Anger: A Sign Someone Cares

Let us start with our own human experience of anger, whilst recalling the biblical caveats 'I am God, and no mortal' (Hosea 11.9), 'my thoughts and not your thoughts' (Isaiah 55.8). Human experience can, presumably, be a guide to understanding what the Bible means by God's wrath since two common biblical images of God are those of a parent and a husband.

An early experience of mine in school teaching will illustrate a crucial point. I taught for a short time at an inner-city school in Birmingham. The boys were not always easy to discipline, but I was fortunate in having a very fine teacher as a close colleague. He once explained to me why it was sometimes right and even helpful to get angry with the boys: the teacher's anger was a sign of his concern and care. But — equally crucially — the teacher never (one hopes!) loses his temper.

The book of Psalms in the Old Testament refers sometimes to God's anger, as in Psalm 6.1 ('O Lord do not rebuke me in your anger...'). A recent commentator notes, 'his anger is a reflection of his care for the world he is creating...', observing, 'anger, not indifference, is the true expression of concern'.[9] Every good parent knows this. If little Johnny runs out into the road, especially when he really knows better than to do that, a loving parent is naturally angry. Human anger, of course, often reflects our limitations: we've had enough of little Johnny for the time being, and we're just plain tired. Or if 'little Johnny' is actually a strapping teenager who is bigger than we are, we may be angry not just because we care, but because we feel our authority as a parent is being challenged.

In the Bible, God's wrath is the obverse side of God's love. It doesn't always look like that, but that is the only interpretation which ultimately makes sense. So, God's anger is *always* a sign God cares. The word 'almighty', applied to God, has been defined as God's ability never to lose control of himself. But even God, according to the graphic language of Hosea 11.1-9, finds it difficult sometimes not to 'lose his rag' with a wayward people.

So, common to Old and New Testaments alike is the conviction that God's 'wrath' is an expression of his love and concern. But does this explain all biblical material about God's anger? It would appear not, although I think it is the interpretative key to the Bible as a whole. When, however, God's anger annihilates people, as in the stories of the Exodus and the Conquest, it is impossible to argue that it demonstrates how much he cares. We have to conclude that that may be how the writer saw things, but we are not obliged to agree. (On this, see Chapter 2, section 1, 'God the Terrorist', and section 2, '"Divine Massacres", Ancient and Modern'.)

This may seem like picking and choosing: some passages we interpret literally, others we do not. That is true, up to a point. But there are two crucial points to make here. First, God as God really is cannot be simply identified with all the different ways in which God is portrayed in the

Bible. Second, we have to make some overall sense of the Bible's understanding of God in relation to God as God really is. That rules out a God who is schizophrenic or wildly inconsistent. And the Bible insists over and over again that God is nothing if not consistent: heart-warmingly or alarmingly (depending on your viewpoint) consistent.

The Contemporary Relevance of Divine 'Wrath'

Our contemporary world needs to hear the Bible's deeper teaching about the 'wrath' of God. Psalm 90 is a meditation on the transience and fragility of human life before the everlastingness (vv.1-2) and anger (vv.7-12) of God:

> For all our days pass away under your wrath;
> our years come to an end like a sigh (v.9).

At first sight, there seems no connection with God's care here: God simply looms over cowering mortals like a threatening thundercloud. Humankind stands under judgement:

> You have set our iniquities before you... (v.8).

Yet the Psalmist knows this is not the whole truth, as the concluding section to the Psalm shows (vv.13-17).

Another cluster of images will help us to understand more fully the Bible's teaching about the wrath of God. Consider first the Aaronic blessing, familiar to many from its use in church liturgies:

> The Lord bless you and keep you;
> The Lord make his face to shine upon and be gracious to you...
> (Numbers 6.24-25).

The imagery suggests that God's 'face' is the source of illumination for humankind. So, the consequence of God 'hiding his face' is darkness, as the Bible insists. Psalm 27 begins 'The Lord is my light', but the Psalmist goes on to pray 'Do not hide your face from me'.

The same imagery occurs in the prophets:

> ...you have hidden your face from us,
> and have delivered us into the hand of our iniquity (Isaiah 64.7).

Yet the same prophet recognized there is a vicious circle — or a downward spiral — involved here: when God 'hides' himself, humankind goes astray:

> But you were angry, and we sinned;
> because you hid yourself, we transgressed (v.5b).

So, God 'hides his face' in response to human sinfulness, and the consequence of that is that the darkness deepens, the light fades still further.[10]

This language and this imagery are difficult for us today. But the truth behind it, I suggest, is important. Whoever or whatever 'God' is, God's withdrawal from the world, or God's absence (if these are the right words) is bad news for the human race. We begin to flounder in a spiritual and moral darkness of our own making.

Divine Love and Wrath

It is a pity that well-meaning but mistaken Christian literalists have brought the Bible into disrepute. Understood literally, some of the Bible's language takes us in the direction of pagan mythologies in which gods unleash their thunderbolts against humans who have offended them.

God's 'judgements' are best understood as part of God's purposive processes at work in human life and history. God's judgements expose the difference between 'light' and 'darkness', truth and illusion, reality and unreality. So, the Bible makes a close connection between the wrath of God and the darkness and unreality of human illusions and idols. If that's where a nation insists on staying, it will be very difficult for it to experience the divine love, simply because such illusions and idols, by their very nature, are always destructive and life-denying.

Of course, if this were all the Bible had to say about God, there would be no gospel. We need to recall our first theme: God's anger is a sign that he cares, not that he has lost his temper, or that he is indifferent. Both human love and human anger may reflect God's love and 'anger', but only — to anticipate later chapters — to the extent that they are free of self-centredness.

All of this means that we cannot, as many still do, simply contrast the Old and New Testaments, as if the God of the Old is a God of wrath, and the God of the New is a God of love. This is to distort both parts of the Christian Bible. The Old Testament again and again proclaims and celebrates God's love, and the New continues at least some of the Old Testament's teaching about wrath. So, we should not airbrush out of our Bibles all those passages in which God's anger occurs. Difficult and unfashionable though the themes of wrath and judgement are these days, they cannot be ignored or rejected without turning God into the equivalent of an indulgent, rather than loving parent.

5. Summary

The Bible's explanation of the destruction of Israel and Judah as independent nations by Assyria and Babylon should not satisfy us. God doesn't 'run' the world like that; the idea that the sun always 'shines on the righteous' didn't fit the facts then — and doesn't now.

The heart-searching experience of the Judaean exiles in Babylon led to a greater understanding of God, a wider vision of the world, and a deeper concept of Israel's own vocation.

The concept of God's 'judgement' is important and necessary: contravening the moral order of God's world may bring disaster. The word 'wrath', like, probably, all the words we use about God, can mislead us. God's anger is best compared to human anger *at its best and most self-possessed*: a sign that someone cares.

6. Looking Ahead

'Where was he, then?', asked the man fiercely, seeing me, a minister of religion. '*Where was he?*' I was startled at this angry question from a total stranger. But I knew what he meant. It was a day or two after the massacre of the children at Beslan in Russia in 2004. He meant '*Where was God?*'

'Why does God allow such things?', 'How can a God of love have made a world with so much suffering, and pain?', and 'What have I done to deserve this?' are questions often heard in the case against God. But if, as the people of the Bible slowly learned, the sun doesn't always shine on the righteous — and the innocent — what other responses might there be to the 'problem' of suffering?

'Mystery' is a better word than 'problem' here, since 'problem' might suggest there is a solution. But what if there isn't? In today's 'developed' world, especially, many people are angry with a God they don't believe in, wanting an explanation to their conundrum: how can a God of love 'allow' suffering — sometimes of horrendous dimensions?

But what if we are framing the question wrongly? What if we are operating with a dubious idea of God as a supernatural being who is supposed to micro-manage the universe? What if there is no such god, and the real God engages with the world he is creating very differently? That, of course, is still a question about God — to answer if we can.

In the Old Testament, Psalm 73 and — in a very different way — the book of Job seem to say that you have to *start* from some kind of faith in God, even if that faith involves swearing at God. The Psalmist wants to know why wicked people often flourish (vv.4-12). The question was clearly eating away at his soul (vv.2-3, 21-22). Eventually, he arrives at a quite different place:

> Whom have I in heaven but you?
> And there is nothing on earth that I desire other than you (v.25).

On the human level, there is a commitment which precedes even belief in God, and that's a commitment in life to compassion and sacrifice and love. 'If we decide against love, God ceases to be even remotely plausible.'[11] So, how we respond to suffering, whether our own or someone else's, is what matters most. Greater self-knowledge, forgiveness and compassion, for instance, are better than bitterness or self-centredness. But that's easier said than done.

I return to this subject in section 3, 'An Elusive, Cruel(?) "You"', and in section 6, 'Looking Ahead', in the next chapter.

* * *

Three Questions for Reflection and Discussion

1 Could the exile in Babylon have been God's punishment of his people? And if not, how are we to understand the authority of biblical books like Jeremiah and Ezekiel?

2 How true is the thought that good may come out of suffering? Is what we do with our suffering an acid test of our faith?

3 Are the Bible's themes of God's judgements and wrath necessary for understanding the world as God's world? Or are they too difficult and even dangerous?

Going Deeper: Further Reading

Walter Brueggemann, *Hopeful Imagination: Prophetic Voices in Exile* (Fortress, 1986).

Henry McKeating, *The Book of Jeremiah* (Epworth/SCM, 1999).

Michael Thompson, *Where is the God of Justice? The Old Testament and Suffering* (Wipf & Stock, 2011).

Endnotes

1   The name 'Israel' is used in the Bible in two ways: it can refer to the whole nation — in this sense, *God's* people — or to the northern kingdom (of Israel) after the political division following the death of Solomon. 'Judah' was the southern kingdom's name.

2   2 Chronicles is almost certainly a re-write of 2 Kings.

3   H. McKeating, *The Book of Jeremiah* (Epworth, 1999), p.15. See also M. Thompson's *Where is the God of Justice? The Old Testament and Suffering* (Wipf & Stock, 2011).

4   McKeating, *The Book of Jeremiah*, p.15.

5   M. Thompson, *Isaiah 40–66* (Epworth, 2001), p.15.

6   L. Stulman, *Jeremiah* (Abingdon, 2005), p.23.

7   H. Butterfield, *Writings on Christianity and History* (Oxford University Press, 1979), pp.86-87.

8   H. Mowvley, *The Books of Amos and Hosea* (Epworth, 1991), p.155.

9   R. Davidson, *The Vitality of Worship: A Commentary on the Book of Psalms* (Eerdmans, 1998) p.30.

10 See my *God in the New Testament* (Epworth, 1999), pp.63-87.

11 J.A. Baker, *The Foolishness of God* (Darton, Longman & Todd, 1970), p.68.

4

'God Is a "You" Rather than an "It"'

The God of the Bible is a God of people, rather than of places.

The Bible's story is a kind of conversation between God and humankind whose component parts have been told and re-told; re-cycled, edited and re-edited. So, the Bible offers its readers a conversation to take part in, a world for them imaginatively to step inside. Believing six impossible things before breakfast is not one of the preliminary requirements. But being prepared to let go of preconceived ideas will certainly help the conversation. With or without faith, to read it attentively, with an open mind and heart, is a good start.

From the very beginning of the Bible God is presented as an outgoing God. No splendid Olympian isolation for God here. (Not that the divine residents of Mount Olympus in Greek mythology kept themselves to themselves; they were forever intervening in human affairs — interventions which usually lacked all consistency or morality.) Instead, God in the Bible brings into being a world and relates to humankind with a consistency of purpose which both disturbs and heartens, unsettles and encourages.

God's *forte* is *relating*: God is a 'You', rather than an 'It'. So, the God of
the Bible is a God of people, rather than of places. As the Bible's story
unfolds, it becomes clear that you can't pin this God down — not even to
Jerusalem. This was just as well, in view of what Nebuchadnezzar's armies
did to Jerusalem in 586 BCE. According to the prophet Ezekiel, God got
out just in time — and 'lived to fight another day'. (What Ezekiel actually
says — Ezekiel 10 — is that God's 'glory' left the Temple.) Even though,
in subsequent centuries, people continued to talk of 'the house of God'
being in Jerusalem, that was not to be the Bible's last word on the subject.[1]

As we have seen, all kinds of ghastly actions are attributed to God in
this developing story of God in relation to humankind. God, again and
again, acts — often 'fights' — on behalf of Israel at the expense of other
nations. Taken at face value, these stories raise troubling questions about
God, and I have suggested that they be read differently. That applies also
to Israel's experience of exile. The prophets, naturally perhaps, interpreted
this catastrophe as God's punishment, but that is another problematic
interpretation which I have questioned in Chapter 3.

In view of all this, is it possible to say something more positive and
attractive about the character of God in the Old Testament? I shall argue
that it is, and so this chapter will

- ask what the Bible means when it calls God 'righteous' and
  'holy',

- explore what the God of the Bible has to do with everyday life,

- discover what one of the Bible's most subversive books, the
  book of Job, has to say about God,

- dip into the Psalms to sketch a personal profile of God.

This chapter will be the last one in this book which focuses on the Old Testament. So, we shall also be making connections with the New Testament as we go along, in order to pave the way for what follows.

1. An Awesomely Consistent 'You'

A 'Righteous' God

When we try to hear what the Bible is saying about God, one of our biggest problems is the language. Some of the Bible's key words are particularly difficult for modern readers. In this section we look at two of them.

Old Testament writers never tire of saying that God is 'righteous', and acts with 'righteousness'. These English words are old-fashioned, if not archaic, but they are still the best for translating the original Hebrew and Greek words. The modern expression 'self-righteous' makes it even harder to understand what they mean, but they are too important to ignore.

In the Bible God's righteousness is God's consistency. If we ask 'consistent in what?', the answer is 'consistent in being God, consistent in character, will and purpose'. Many psalms reflect this conviction: for example,

> Hear my prayer, O Lord;
> give ear to my supplications in your faithfulness;
> answer me in your righteousness...
> For your name's sake, O Lord, preserve my life.
> In your righteousness bring me out of trouble (Psalm 143.1, 11).

The GNB reverses 'faithfulness' and 'righteousness' in v.1 and in v.11 translates the Hebrew word for 'righteousness' as 'goodness'. The translation isn't wrong; it shows how God's righteousness *is* his faithfulness and goodness, although even that doesn't quite do justice to God's consistency.

So, God is utterly consistent in both his commitment to human beings, and to the 'order' of his creation. That is God's righteousness, which undergirds, according to the Bible, human well-being, the well-being of creation and its moral order — all three.

God's Consistency in 'Judging' and 'Saving'

It's difficult to exaggerate the importance of God's 'righteousness' in the Bible. But the contemporary associations of the word are unfortunate. It sounds narrowly moralistic, as if God polices the universe like a cosmic moralist, or an eternally vigilant judge. There *is* a dimension of judgement, as there is bound to be if God is consistent. (On the theme of judgment, see Chapter 3, section 3, 'The "Judgements" of God in History'.) But because God's righteousness denotes all that God is and does, it is often associated with other key biblical words, like 'salvation'.

Two of the later prophets of the Old Testament show this especially clearly. Both stood in the tradition of Isaiah, and so the edited prophecies of both are included in the book of Isaiah, at chapters 40–55 and 56–66. The first of these prophets ('Second' Isaiah), whose prophecies we encountered in the last chapter, assured the downcast exiles in Babylon of a new 'exodus' for them. When that happens, they will see how God's 'righteousness' and 'salvation' go together:

Shower, O heavens, from above,

and let the skies rain down righteousness;

let the earth open, that salvation may spring up (Isaiah 45.8a).

The New Testament picks up the same theme: God's righteousness is the consistency of God. He is unwaveringly committed to human well-being, the well-being of creation and its moral order.

God's Righteousness and Human Responsibility

This may begin to sound like a dynasty of English kings, but scholars have identified a 'Third Isaiah' (Trito-Isaiah), a disciple of Second Isaiah whose expanded and edited prophecies comprise Isaiah 56–66. There is a double reference to righteousness in the very first verse, Isaiah 56.1, though this is not apparent in translations. Translated literally, the verse includes a command and a promise which say 'Maintain righteousness… and my righteousness will be revealed'. We might paraphrase: if humans start putting right what is wrong, they will find that God does the same. God, however, according to the Bible, doesn't just reciprocate; he takes the initiative, as St Paul insists in his Letter to the Romans (Romans 1.16-17; 3.21-26).

Holy as Thou?

There is another problem word deeply rooted in the Bible's story about God. This is the word 'holiness'. These days we find it hard to define holiness, though many people know a holy person when they see one, and we might be conscious of a 'holy' place, such as an ancient church where prayer has been offered for centuries. But just as 'righteous' is tainted by 'self-righteous', so 'holy' may be tainted by the expression 'holier than thou'.

Many of us were taught that God's holiness is God's 'otherness', God's separateness from human contamination. But that's only part of the picture. God in the Bible is outgoing and relational. But to say that God is 'holy' means that God, in all his outgoing-ness, is never compromised or contaminated. In this respect, God's holiness and righteousness — his consistency and integrity in relationships — belong together.

These fundamental qualities of God have far-reaching implications for human life. God not only commits himself to the well-being and order of creation, but invites humans into partnership with him in doing this. Many texts in the Bible show the close connection between God's character and how things are going in the human world, as in this prophecy from Isaiah 5.15-16:

> People are bowed down, everyone is brought low.
> and the eyes of the haughty are humbled.
> But the Lord of hosts is exalted by justice,
> and the Holy God shows himself holy by righteousness.

A Two-Edged Sword

So, to borrow a biblical image, God's holiness, like God's righteousness, is a 'two-edged sword'. The divine title 'the Holy One of Israel' can preface a word either of judgement or of salvation, as in Isaiah 30.12-15:

> Therefore thus says the Holy One of Israel:
>
> Because you reject this word,
>
> and put your trust in oppression and deceit...
>
> therefore this iniquity shall become for you
>
> like a break in a high wall...
>
> whose crash comes suddenly, in an instant... (vv.12-13)

But then,

> For thus said the Lord God, the Holy One of Israel:
>
> In returning and rest you shall be saved (v.15a).

We looked at the concept of judgement in human life and history in the previous chapter, and we shall need to return to it when we come to the New Testament. As for the link between God's holiness and salvation, that becomes especially prominent in the later prophecies of Second Isaiah (Isaiah 40–55). A new note is sounded here: the assertion that your 'redeemer' is the Holy One of Israel:

> Do not fear, you worm Jacob,
>
> you insect Israel!
>
> I will help you, says the Lord;
>
> your redeemer is the Holy One of Israel (Isaiah 41.14 — one of many occurrences of this description of God in Isaiah 40–55).

In these chapters God's 'salvation' takes the form of deliverance from exile in Babylon, with international consequences. The final prophecy of Second Isaiah recapitulates the themes of earlier ones:

...nations that do not know you shall run to you,

because of the Lord your God, the Holy One of Israel,

for he has glorified you (Isaiah 55.5).

The Contagion of Holiness

So, contrary to what modern connotations of the word might suggest, God's holiness isn't something God keeps to himself. That's not true of either the Old or the New Testament, which recounts the gift of God's Holy Spirit even to Gentiles, unclean and impure though they were supposed to be. (Simon Peter's dream about a tablecloth and the sequel to it in Acts 10 makes the point. See also 'Jesus in Bad Company' in Chapter 5, section 3, 'Not a God for Religious People'.)

A contemporary theologian, Wolfhart Pannenberg, has suggested that God's purpose is to bring the whole world into the sphere of divine holiness by entering the world and transforming it. In the end, the divine holiness, so far from confining itself to a 'holy of holies' in a sacred building, spreads far and wide.

An important reason why this is so is that God's holiness isn't simply awesome — as in Isaiah's vision in the Temple (Isaiah 6.1-8) — it is also attractive. The holiness of God is the beauty of God. To see that beauty is the Psalmist's great passion in life (Psalm 27.4). To say God is 'beautiful' is to say that God has 'this power of attraction which speaks for itself'.[2]

As often in the Bible, characteristics of God are meant to be replicated in humans. Israel is repeatedly told, 'Be holy, for I am holy' (Leviticus 11.44-45; 19.2; 20.7, 26). But if God's holiness may also be called the beauty of God, that command isn't as unattractive and austere as it sounds. Suffice to say for now that the close connection in the Bible between holiness, justice and compassion shows that it's worlds away from what the expression 'holier than thou' might suggest.

All in all, there is an awesome consistency about the 'You' whose 'story' the Bible tells. In the Psalmist 's words, 'good and upright is the Lord' (Psalm 25.8a). 'This means that God is straight and above board in all his dealings'.[3] That might suggest a harsh, unbending morality, but the same psalm spells out a rather different consequence of God's 'upright-ness':

> *therefore* he instructs sinners in the way (v.8b).

So, God in his consistency (God's righteousness and holiness) is deeply committed to his creation — even when the human section of it goes off-course. These themes continue in the New Testament. The baptism of Jesus will 'fulfil' God's righteousness (Matthew 3.15), and a disciple will call him 'the Holy One of God' (John 6.69). But as the story of Jesus will show, a consistent God will be anything but boring and predictable.

2. The Always and Everywhere 'You'

The Danger of a 'Spiritual' Religion

In the Bible God is more 'earthy' and less 'religious' than most of us — religious and unreligious alike — often realize. Most ordained ministers of the Church will be familiar with this opening line in a conversation: 'Well, I'm not religious...' People who say that may not realize how anti-religious the Bible often is. True, the Bible affirms genuine religion (as in Micah 6.8 and James 1.27), but it is very severe on empty, hypocritical religion. What is more, it's surprisingly worldly. It is more accurate to say of the Bible than ever it was of a now defunct Sunday newspaper that 'the whole of human life is there'.

There is a danger of making the Bible too 'spiritual', as if God were more interested in our souls than our bodies, or as if God were pre-occupied with the moral education of humankind and little else. The Bible can be made to sound like that, and the centuries-long tradition of placing the Ten Commandments in every parish church in England (for example) strengthens that impression. But in those days the squire and the vicar were sometimes all too inclined to favour the image of God as a moral policeman as a way of keeping the lower classes in order.

The Bible, in fact, doesn't deal much in the contrasts often heard from Christian pulpits between the material ('bad') and the spiritual ('good'). The word 'spiritual' is rare in the Bible; like 'spirituality', it's difficult to define. So we need to forget the idea that God's main interests are religion and the department of life known as 'the spiritual'. God ought not to be characterized as 'spiritual' in contrast to physical; that's a contrast we read into the Bible.

God's canvas is far broader than religion and 'the spiritual'. According to the Bible, God commits himself to the wellbeing of his creation. That, of course, includes humankind whom God has endowed as 'centers of power genuinely other than God's power, yet dependent on God for their reality and value'.[4]

A Monday God

There is also a long — and misguided — Christian tradition that ordinary, everyday life distracts us from God. It can, of course, but religion and daily life are not in competition with each other. People who have written about what I would call authentic spirituality emphasize how believing in God means giving more not less attention to what each moment brings.

Much Christian thinking has been skewed by starting from the idea that the Creator originally made a perfect world (Genesis 1 and 2), and we humans messed up (Genesis 3). So, the best thing religious people can do, so the argument goes, is to avoid getting too entangled in 'the world'; a semi-detached stance is best: 'in the world, not of it'.

This is a serious misreading of the Bible. The God to whom the Bible bears witness is God of creation and life in all their extraordinary variety and wonder. Creation is one of the Bible's central themes. The Bible also has a lot to say about everyday life, particularly in its so-called Wisdom literature (Job, Proverbs, Ecclesiastes and — in the Apocrypha — Ecclesiasticus and the Wisdom of Solomon).

So, in thinking about the Bible's understanding of God, we should give prominence to the words 'creation', 'life' and 'human'. Then, what being 'religious' and 'spiritual' involves is likely to get an answer more in keeping with the Bible.

'The Glory of God is a Human Being Fully Alive'

This much-quoted saying of the second-century bishop Irenaeus reflects biblical teaching far more than modern secular definitions of freedom. The 'glory' of human beings — so closely related in the Bible to God's glory — does not consist in getting behind or beyond everyday life and back to a lost paradise. Similarly, human freedom doesn't lie in somehow rising above everyday life in a haze of spiritual transcendence. The Bible counsels against bypassing everyday life as if that were the only way to realize the Kingdom of God. Contrary to modern post-enlightenment ideas, God is the key to human freedom and glory; without God, paradoxically, that freedom and glory easily become less than human.

This may seem a far cry from our question 'who is God?', but, in the biblical view, this is not so. Even though the Bible insists that God's ways and thoughts are higher than our ways and thoughts (Isaiah 55.9), the question of God and the question of humankind are mysteriously and deeply interrelated. So, faith in God is bound up closely with the everyday. Faith is the attitude of trust in all that the Creator gives here and now, even when, as the Bible recognizes, protests to God are perfectly in order.

God's Delight in Creation

There is much in the Old Testament which is deeply life-affirming because life is seen as the good gift of the creator God. A few examples must suffice. First, we note the Psalmists' insistence that God enjoys or delights in his creation:

> May the Lord rejoice in his works... (Psalm 104.31b)

> ...his compassion is over all that he has made (Psalm 145.9b; compare Ecclesiastes 5.18-20 on human enjoyment).

The Old Testament sometimes pictures God's involvement with the world by speaking of God's 'wisdom', as here in the book of Proverbs:

> ...when he marked out the foundations of the earth,
>
> then I (i.e. Wisdom) was beside him, like a master worker;
>
> and I was daily his delight,
>
> rejoicing before him always,
>
> rejoicing in his inhabited world
>
> and delighting in the human race (Proverbs 8.29c-31).

Just as divine and human glory are mysteriously connected, so God's wisdom is the key to human wisdom, as a poem in the book of Job shows (Job 28, especially vv.12-13, 23 and 28).

Because the Bible affirms life and creation, and the importance of wisdom, it's also very practical. Humans must take ordinary everyday life seriously; for example

> Know well the condition of your flocks,
>
> And give attention to your herds;
>
> For riches do not last forever... (Proverbs 27.23).

The Psalms, especially, have a lively sense that a human life doesn't last forever (e.g. Psalms 39.4-6, 11-13). To this the New Testament adds the conviction that this life is not all there is, though this was a belief beginning to surface in the latest books of the Old Testament, such as Daniel.

All Good Gifts

The book of Exodus offers an attractive example of the ubiquitous Creator Spirit. The church of which I was the minister once held what we called a 'day of many colours'. We designated as its 'patron saint' an obscure character in the book of Exodus called Bezalel. We chose him because Bezalel was a master craftsman, 'filled…with divine spirit, with skill, intelligence and knowledge in every kind of craft, to devise artistic designs…in gold, silver, and bronze, in cutting stones for setting, and in carving wood…' (Exodus 35.31-32).

As I have said, there is a long tradition in Christianity of denigrating the material and the physical, and in the process distorting our under-standing of God. That is odd, given the amount of time which, according to the Gospels, Jesus of Nazareth devoted to healing human bodies. So, the Old Testament's life-affirming themes are important. 'God saw everything that he had made, and indeed, it was very good' (Genesis 1.31). That cannot mean 'once upon a time, in some lost Eden', even though the world's full potential for goodness has yet to be realized.

This 'down-to-earth-ness' of the Bible, in the Christian view, comes to a climax in the human being whom one Gospel calls 'the Word (i.e. of God) made flesh' (John 1.14). It's a far cry from the lord of the manor coming down to earth to show a bit of solidarity with mere mortals. In the story the Gospels tell, this God on earth will disappear for three whole days, and the world be engulfed in darkness, before the light of God's consistency breaks through once more.

Even then, questions, doubts and suffering remain. The God repre-sented in the Bible does not solve every problem or protect 'the righteous' from all harm. It's not like that at all, as the Psalmists and the writer of the book of Job knew full well.

3. An Elusive, Cruel(?) 'You'

God in the Bible can be exasperatingly elusive — even disappointing. So, 'crying' to God is one way to pray. Cries to God occur in Old and New Testament alike. Afflicted people cry through Jesus to God; Jesus on the cross cries out to God, echoing Psalm 22.1:

> My God, my God why have you forsaken me? (Matthew 27.46; Mark 15.34).

In the Psalms there are other cries; 'wake up!' (44.23), 'rise up!' (3.7), and 'how long, O Lord?' (13.1) are just three of the peremptory commands or questions directed at God. But this elusive God seems to take his time in 'waking up', and then the only thing exasperated people can do is wait (e.g. Psalm 62.1).

The question '*Where* are you?', however, was not a question the Psalmists[5] asked. That was a question for others:

> ...people say to me continually, 'Where is your God?' (42.3).

It was a question for sceptics to ask when they thought there was no 'You' to see what they were getting up to (e.g. Psalm 94.7).

But in the Bible people who complain to God don't give up. Like characters in stories told by Jesus, they go on making a nuisance of themselves. The Bible is realistic but always hopeful about an elusive God. That elusiveness (if that is the right word) helps to explain why, especially in the Old Testament, people are not always polite in what they say about God or even in what they say to God. The book of Job, perhaps the most subversive in the whole Bible, provides a prime example.

Job and His 'Religious' Friends

The story of Job is quickly outlined, since there is a story only at the very beginning and end of the book (chapters 1–2 and 42). 'Satan' (not to be confused with the devil) is given permission by God to test Job, a prosperous, happy, devout man. Will Job still be devout when all his prosperity and happiness have gone? First, Job loses his oxen and donkeys (1.14-15), next his sheep and shepherds (1.16), then his camels (1.17), his sons and daughters (1.18-19) and, finally, his own health (2.7).

In the chapters which follow Job's friends talk to him about God. It all sounds very pious and religious: what you would expect in the circumstances, given their belief that Job's afflictions must be the result of Job's wrongdoing. Thus Eliphaz (Job's 'comforter' no.1) leads off:

> Can mortals be righteous before God?...
> ...therefore do not despise the discipline of the Almighty (4.17a; 5.17b).

There is more of the same from comforter no.2, Bildad (8.2, 5-6), and a rather angrier comforter no.3, Zophar (11.4-6). Comforter no.1 returns to the charge (15.4, 8) and comforter no.2 with a lecture on the fate of the wicked (18.5-21).

But how does anyone answer questions like these:

> Have you listened in the council of God?
> And do you limit wisdom to yourself? (15.8; compare vv.7-16).

Enter comforter no.4, Elihu, who is given more lines than the other three put together (chapters 32–37). He's angry not only with Job, but also with his three friends because they couldn't answer Job (32.2-3). But there is still more of the same from Elihu: Job is 'irreverent' (34.7), and God will repay everyone 'according to their deeds' (34.11).

What are we to make of all this very 'proper', respectful language about God? Some commentators think that Job's criticism of people 'who bring their god in their hands' (12.6) is a reference to his friends. Whether it is or not, their god seems restricted to a law of reward and punishment. So, is this 'god' really sovereign after all? Job goes on to ask them if they 'speak falsely for God' (13.7).

Between the speeches of the first three of his 'comforters' Job gives as good as he gets. In the process, his language about God borders on the blasphemous: God has put him in the wrong (19.6), the wicked and the blasphemous go unpunished (21.1-16), and God himself is both elusive and terrifying (23.3, 8-9, 16). Yet still Job maintains he has done no wrong (e.g. 27.6 and 29.14-17).

God's Reply

But what of God's response in the poem which follows (chapters 38–41), long regarded as one of the masterpieces of literature? God seems to address Job with a megaphone, hurling at him one question after another, beginning with

Where were you when I laid the foundation of the earth? (38.4).

As a famous British comedian used to say, 'There's no answer to that'.

Job's first response to God amounts to, 'No more questions; my lips are sealed' (40.3-5). God, however, has no intention of squashing or humiliating him:

> Gird up your loins like a man;
>
> I will question you, and you declare to me...
>
> Deck yourself with majesty and dignity;
>
> clothe yourself with glory and splendour (40.7, 10).

God's words here recall the description of humankind in Psalm 8.5 as 'a little lower than God, and crowned...with glory and honour'.

So what do the speeches of God in the book of Job actually do? They point to a universe and to a Creator of that universe of which human beings can have only the faintest inkling. It is mysterious, awesome, incomprehensible — even the odd behaviour of the ostrich whom God has caused to 'forget wisdom' (39.13-18) or nature red in tooth and claw (39.29-30). Here, in fact, are poems which invite awe and wonder before the transcendent, creative Power or Being behind all things.

Story's End: God's New World

Some people think that the end of the story is very unsatisfactory, with none of the difficult questions answered at all: a sort of 'happy ever after' ending, with Job's prosperity and happiness restored (42.10-16). But it is more than that. The tables are turned on Job's comforters. For all their pious talk, God isn't pleased with what they've said (42.7). As one commentator remarks, 'God has a healthy mistrust for his more self-assured supporters'.[6]

So, this subversive bit of the Bible disapproves of supposed believers in God who trot out pious clichés in the face of human suffering. It's simply not true to say 'the sun always shines on the righteous'. Life isn't so straightforward, and that, as this book — and other parts of the Old Testament — recognizes, is part of the challenge of believing in God.

As for the ending itself, it's not quite as conventional (in story terms) as it might first appear. What God in his generosity now gives Job is not so much reward for his behaviour, as a reward for praying for his so-called friends (42.7-10). God gives Job a whole new world. It's a world so new that Job's three new daughters — unlike, apparently their seven brothers — are given names, and also equal property rights with their brothers. And all this in a patriarchal world. We might reasonably conclude: subversive to the end!

But is God cruel, as well as elusive? It sometimes seems so, and the story of Job neither shirks the question nor offers easy answers. It doesn't provide an 'answer' to the problems of suffering and of evil as we observe and experience them. But this isn't the Bible's last word on these subjects. I return to the 'problem' of suffering in section 6, 'Looking Ahead', at the end of the chapter, and in subsequent chapters.

4. 'My God', 'Our God'

Like every word we use of God, the word 'personal' can be mis-understood. The Bible doesn't portray a personal God with whom one may be 'chummy'. God can't be reduced to a person, not even a superhuman person. So, the Bible discourages a familiarity which takes God for granted, but at the same time it gives eloquent expression to an intimacy with God. God is always the ever-present 'You', never an 'It':

> O Lord you have searched me and known me.
> You know when I sit down and when I rise up;
> you discern my thoughts from far away (Psalm 139.1-2).

So, first, in this section, we must look at the Bible's more personal language about God and addressed to God.

'My God'

The Old Testament books from Joshua to 2 Kings (the 'Deuteronomistic History') might give the impression that God is concerned only with the big picture: the fate of nations and empires, and with those individuals most responsible for that fate, namely, monarchs and prophets. Some of the psalms also review the fortunes of the nation and celebrate or pray for the well-being of the king (e.g. Psalms 45, 72, 110). In many psalms, however, we have not 'our God' but 'my God':

> O God, you are my God, I seek you,
>
> my soul thirsts for you... (Psalm 63.1a).

Recurring themes occur. 'My God' is the object of my passionate longing (Psalms 42.1-2; 84.10), the ground, 'the Rock' on which I rest (Psalm 62.2, 6), the One whose presence is its own reward (Psalms 16.11; 73.25, 28), the source of deepest joy (Psalm 63.5), and the very essence of life. God's 'steadfast love and faithfulness' are the constant backdrop, the ever-present environment in which I live out my life. My God is my 'delight' (Psalms 37.4; 40.8).

'My God' is also a source of unfailing truth and light (Psalms 25.5; 27.1). His 'works' — creation (Psalm 104.31), the Exodus, the gift of the land (Psalm 105.5-15), and personal deliverance (Psalm 116) — are a constant source of wonder and praise. His laws are the staple diet of my life, reviving, making me wise and glad, enlightening me as I go on my way (Psalm 19.7-9), and the recurring theme of the blockbuster Psalm 119 (with its 176 verses).

Many psalms celebrate both God's intimacy and God's transcendence, as in Psalm 113 (and other parts of the Old Testament, e.g. Isaiah 57.15):

Who is like the Lord our God,

who is seated on high,

who looks far down

on the heavens and the earth?

He raises the poor from the dust,

and lifts the needy from the ash heap... (vv.5-7).

'Our God'

For all God's unwavering commitment to his creation, God is not at anyone's beck and call. God is supremely free: always and everywhere, consistently God. But this God, especially in the Old Testament, is often 'our God', a simple expression which raises a number of questions. 'Our God'? Is 'our' here exclusive? Possessive? Triumphalist? How should we interpret it, especially in the light of contemporary religious terrorism?

In the Bible, God chose 'us' (whoever 'we' are), before 'we' chose God. Does this ease the problem? Actually, it could make things better or worse: better, because 'we' were mere nobodies, 'Pharaoh's slaves in Egypt' (Deuteronomy 6.21), until God found us, so we've nothing to brag about. But God choosing 'us' could make things worse, since God's choice might make us feel superior to everyone else. It all depends on what God's choice of us actually means, *and* what it means for everyone else.

It's relevant here to ask how an identity — whether a person's or a nation's — is forged. Human difference plays a huge part. So does arguing, especially between young siblings. But that isn't the whole picture. The identities of two people married to each other don't develop through constant fighting. Arguments play their part, but love plays an even more important part.

Similarly, nations and religions don't have to fight in order to establish their own traditions and identities.

So, when a group — Jewish, Christian or Muslim — says 'our God', what matters is the spirit in which they say it, and their attitude to all those not included in that little word 'our'. And this takes us back to the character and purpose of 'our' God.

According to one psalm, God does whatever he pleases (Psalm 135.6). That sounds like the worst kind of autocrat. But, having created an entire world, what actually *does* 'our God' want to do? According to another psalm, this is the God who

> executes justice for the oppressed;
> who gives food to the hungry.
> The Lord sets the prisoners free;
> the Lord opens the eyes of the blind.
> The Lord lifts up those who are bowed down;
> the Lord loves the righteous.
> The Lord watches over the strangers;
> he upholds the orphan and the widow,
> but the way of the wicked he brings to ruin (Psalm 146.7-9).[7]

Does God actually do all this, or is this just a pious hope? One thing we can say in the light of the Bible: in fulfilling his 'programme', God looks for co-operation from the humans he has put in charge (Genesis 1.27-28; Psalm 8.5-8), and particularly from Israel, with her responsibility to show the same compassion as God (Deuteronomy 24.19-22).

Would or can human beings do this without God? That's the big question. The Bible is clear: divine agency and human agency are not mutually exclusive, and a partnership with humankind was the Creator's intention from the beginning.

As the Old Testament section of this book draws to a close, we observe both that God seems to have a long way to go, and also that there are hints of more to come from God: a new covenant (Jeremiah 31.31-34), a new temple (Ezekiel 40–47), the restoration of David's kingdom (Amos 8.11-15), a day of God's vengeance (Isaiah 61.2), a feast of food 'for all peoples' (Isaiah 25.6), a promise of God's spirit 'on all flesh' (Joel 2.28-29), peace among the nations (Micah 4.1-4) — and these are just some of the references.

The hopes and dreams are many and varied, but all of them suggest that the Creator, in spite of all the setbacks, hasn't given up just yet. The promise stands.

But what of 'the nations'? So much of the Old Testament seems to contrast Israel with everyone else. Yet, as we saw in the last chapter, the picture of the nations isn't always a negative one. Even so, it is no exaggeration to say that, in the New Testament, the biblical panorama is transformed.

So, does the Bible offer any hope for the future of planet earth? The stakes are high. Humans can and do add to the destructive chaos which has no part in the purpose of the Creator. Their idolatries damage both themselves and the earth. But the Bible's message about God and 'the nations' suggests that, in our age of globalization, its time has finally come. Crucially — as the Bible ultimately makes clear — the word 'our' in the phrase 'our God' must include everyone.

5. Summary

The divine 'You' so central to the Bible is 'righteous': utterly consistent in character, relationships and in keeping his promises. God is also 'holy': uniquely God, even when God involves himself in the world for the sake of his people Israel: a Reality who can't be compromised or contaminated.

God as the Bible sees God is not God of the 'spiritual' only, as if that were a special 'religious' sector of life. God is God of the everyday, and the Bible surprisingly down-to-earth.

Yet God can be exasperatingly elusive, and seem even hostile or cruel. The book of Job shows that a threatened, angry human being is 'allowed' to protest vigorously; honesty is better than pious clichés.

God, for all his elusiveness, is still the ever-present 'You': life's deepest joy, 'my God' and 'our God'. And that ultimate joy aims to include all the nations of the world.

All these themes, in the Christian view, converge in one life, death and resurrection in a kind of 'fulfilment'. So, in Interlude 2 a brief look at how the Old and New Testaments 'fit' together may be useful before we turn to the story of Jesus.

6. Looking Ahead

We resume the discussion we began at the end of Chapter 3 on the 'problem' of suffering. In the earlier discussion, I suggested that we use the word 'mystery' instead of 'problem', because a 'problem' invites a 'solution', and perhaps neither life nor the world are quite so simple. But that still leaves plenty of reasons for people to be angry with the Creator.

The book of Job is the Bible's deepest engagement with this question. Some of its language is extraordinary; Job 7.7-21 is an incredibly rude and angry prayer. There is more of the same later on (16.6-17), where Job insists his prayer is 'pure'! The prayer of Mary Craig, the mother of a child with Hohler's Syndrome, gargoylism, was angry, too:

> Damn you, you don't exist, but I hate you... All right, if you do exist, show me a way out. For a start, what the hell am I to do next?

Cyril Rodd, who quotes this prayer, suggests that 'the need to be honest with oneself and to talk honestly to God is perhaps the most pressing — and healing — of all'.[8] In two of the four Gospels, the final words of Jesus sound like an angry prayer:

> My God, my God, why have you forsaken me? (Matthew 27.46; Mark 15.34).

But here is an extraordinary paradox. According to the New Testament, this tortured, God-forsaken figure actually *is* God. We'll return to the 'problem' of suffering again, but for now, we note just two things. For Job, this life was all there was; in the New Testament, the resurrection of Christ gives birth to belief in an 'eternal' life beyond death. That belief should *not* invite the bland response: 'So that makes everything all right, then'. But it does put the mystery of suffering in a new perspective.

The last thing is this: there is no intellectual argument in the world which 'solves' the problem of suffering. What does remain, however, is a choice and a sort of 'wager'. We can make a choice for compassion as a good which is even more important than freedom from pain. We can also decide (this is the wager), to 'back life's scent against its stink'. (I'm quoting here Geoffrey Studdart-Kennedy, a chaplain in the trenches of World War 1.)

Trust in God throughout the Bible is always a trust 'in spite of', a faith against the odds. Testimony, experience and, perhaps, growing evidence all suggest there is more to be said for a personal 'You' at the heart of everything than is commonly allowed — in spite of everything.

* * *

Three Questions for Reflection and Discussion

1   'Whatever the Lord pleases he does' (Psalm 135.6). Is this really true, and, if it is, does it sound — in the light of the Bible as a whole — like a promise or a threat?
2   If we can't finally explain the mystery of suffering, is our response to suffering, whether ours or other people's, a way to find the 'elusive' God?
3   Can the expression 'our God' include everyone?

Going Deeper: Further Reading

Adrian Curtis, *Psalms* (Epworth/SCM, 2004).

C.S. Rodd, *The Book of Job* (Epworth/SCM, 1990).

Jonathan Sacks, *Faith in the Future* (Darton, Longman & Todd, 1995).

Endnotes

1   New Testament writers equate, first, Jesus, and then a church with God's Temple (John 2.20-21; 1 Corinthians 3.16).

2   K. Barth, *Church Dogmatics*, II.1, pp.650-51.

3   R. Davidson, *The Vitality of Worship* (Eerdmans, 1998), p.91.

4   D. Kelsey, *Eccentric Existence: A Theological Anthropology* (Westminster John Knox Press, 2009), vol. I, p.256.

5   Although tradition attributed the Psalms to King David, scholarship over many decades now has shown that they come from different authors over several centuries.

6   C.S. Rodd, *The Book of Job* (Epworth/SCM, 1990), p.127, quoting J.C.L. Gibson. For a recent discussion of the book of Job see also M. Thompson's *Where is the God of Justice? The Old Testament and Suffering* (Wipf & Stock, 2011).

7   Here God is portrayed as fulfilling the role 'traditionally associated with he monarch, of caring for those who cannot protect themselves' (A. Curtis, *Psalms* [Epworth, 2004], p.261)

8   Rodd, *The Book of Job*, p.108.

Interlude (2)

Is the God of the Old Testament Different from the God of the New?

This is a natural question to ask, but not an easy one to answer. I have suggested that 'God' as God is portrayed in the texts of the Bible can't be exactly equated with God as God really is. Yet for Christians the Bible speaks in a uniquely authoritative way about God.

First, a bit of history about the Christian Bible. I put it like that because the writings of 'the Old Testament' were the Scriptures of the Jewish people, before the first Christians adopted them as their own as well. (They still are the Bible of Judaism.) Over the next few centuries the Church gradually came to a mind about those Christian writings which should comprise 'the New Testament'. Together, the two Testaments are the Christian Bible.[1]

The Church neglects the Old Testament at its peril. An Old Testament scholar once cited Nazi Germany as an example of how the New Testament can easily be distorted without the Old. Another suggested that the Church would have responded far more effectively to the atheism of the twentieth century if it had not neglected the Old Testament.

But the relationship between the Old and the New is not a simple one. St Augustine, in a famous epigram, wrote,

> The New Testament lies hidden (*latet*) in the Old, the Old Testament is made plain (*patet*) in the New.

I find that illuminating, but it still leaves us with many questions about God as God is portrayed in the Bible.

We need to hold two ideas in tension. First, the Church has always believed that Jesus 'fulfilled' the Scriptures. Yet there is no neat 'fit' between the Old and New Testaments, no seamless transition. The Hebrew Scriptures did not predict Jesus, as is sometimes asserted. That confuses later interpretation of them with their original meaning and purpose.

For example, there is no clear profile of a 'Messiah', although, at Christmas and Easter, the Church naturally finds in Christ the fulfilment of passages such as Isaiah 7.14 ('the young woman is with child'), Isaiah 9.6 ('a child has been born for us'), and Isaiah 53 (e.g. v.5, 'he was wounded for our transgressions'). In fact, no-one predicted — or, perhaps, could have predicted — the Messiah who, Christians believe, eventually came.

So, there is continuity — a profound continuity — between the Old and the New. But it's not a complete or unbroken continuity with no real change. If that were so, presumably Jews and Christians would not have diverged in the way they have. So, to pose the question rather starkly, how different is the God of the Old Testament from the God of the New?

We should reject simplistic contrasts. It's wrong to think of the God of the Old Testament as a god of wrath and law, and the God of the New as a God of love and grace. God's love and grace pervade the Old Testament, and God's wrath and law (differently understood) are to be found in the New. At the risk of over-simplifying, the God of Abraham, Isaac and Jacob is the God and Father of our Lord Jesus Christ.

Yet the centre of gravity shifts. Or, rather, the New Testament has two centres of gravity, not one: not just 'the Lord God', but — as most of the opening greetings of the New Testament letters show — God *and* Jesus. That's the difference between the Old and the New: God now has 'a Son'. (What that means we shall need to explore.)

It might be argued that the New Testament has three 'centres of gravity': 'Father, Son and Holy Spirit' (e.g. Matthew 28.19; 2 Corinthians 13.13). But that, I think, would be to anticipate a little. The Holy Spirit is not as pervasive and prominent in New Testament writings as God and Jesus.

There are other changes of emphasis and perspective as we move from the Old to the New. In exploring these, we should take care not to mis-represent the Old. For example, whereas the Old Testament distinguishes between Israel and 'the nations', the New highlights the difference between the Church and 'the world'. That is not a simple contrast between an exclusive and an inclusive religion, but two perspectives both of which, in different ways, are exclusive and inclusive at the same time.

So, the Old and New Testaments belong together. To put this another way, Jews and Christians are closely related, and it is to be hoped that the third millennium of Christian history will be infinitely better for Jewish–Christian relations than the first two were. The two faiths may yet enrich each other.

As for the Christian Bible as a whole, if we are to interpret well what it has to say about God, we must heed St Augustine's epigram, and allow the two Testaments to illuminate each other.

Endnote

1   In some Bibles, especially Roman Catholic Bibles, there are also additional Jewish writings, known as 'The Apocrypha'. Protestant Christians, however, unlike Catholics, do not usually regard the Apocrypha as part of their Scriptures.

5

Jesus and God

The Resurrection...is the divine signature across the life,
teaching and death of Jesus.

What difference does Jesus make to biblical teaching about God? Some of his teaching and actions offended religious people, and his death was an even greater religious scandal: a 'son of God' abandoned by God (Matthew 27.46; Mark 15.34), even 'cursed' by God (Deuteronomy 21.23; Galatians 3.13). Later, after Jesus' humiliating death, his disciples claimed they saw him again, and that God had raised him from the dead. If *that* was true, what did that say about God?

So, this chapter will

- begin at the end, asking what the resurrection of Jesus says about God's character,

- explore the extraordinary things Jesus said about God, including the difficult references to eternal punishment,

- ask why he offended religious people so much that they wanted to kill him,

- look briefly at the story of the Virgin Birth, and the misunderstandings about it.

1. Jesus and the Question of God

Imagine getting a letter through the post which has no signature at the end. If the handwriting is familiar, or there is an address at the top which you recognize, you can soon work out who is the author of your unsigned letter. If there is neither — you have a mystery on your hands!

Without the resurrection the life and message of Jesus would be like an unsigned letter from God — if, that is, God exists and Jesus spoke the truth about him. After all, Jesus had claimed God sent him. So, his crucifixion, if that really was the end of him, put a huge question-mark against everything he had said about God. The moral teaching of Jesus might still inspire, but the God 'bit' of his teaching — which actually is far more than a 'bit' — becomes a problem.

That is why, in this chapter, we have to begin at the end. In a sense, the writers of the four Gospels in the New Testament did just that. Their belief that there had been a life-changing sequel to the crucifixion coloured everything they wrote. That is hardly surprising, since the resurrection of Jesus Christ now becomes the key to a Christian under-standing of what the Bible says about God. It is the divine signature across the life, teaching and death of Jesus.

Is the Resurrection True?

Michael Licona is a Christian New Testament scholar who recently wrote a book of over 600 pages painstakingly exploring the historical evidence and arguments for the resurrection. The book was the outcome of hours of research over many years. He also examined the arguments against the resurrection: for example, Jesus didn't die, or the disciples stole his body and invented the story of his resurrection. He concluded that, though the resurrection can't be proved from the evidence we have, the arguments explaining it away are not convincing either. For example, the very disciples who are supposed to have stolen Jesus' body seem to have been convinced, along with Paul and many others (1 Corinthians 15.3-8), that the crucified Jesus had appeared to them, so God had raised him from the dead, and this was worth dying for.

The resurrection stories in the Gospels, like most if not all the stories in the Bible, are not straightforward historical accounts. How could they be, when there are so many contradictions and differences? If all of this was meant to be evidence in a courtroom, the counsel for the prosecution would want to know, for example, why the names of the women who went to the tomb are not all the same in Matthew, Mark and Luke, or why the versions in Luke's and John's Gospels of Jesus' first appearance to his disciples vary so much (Luke 24.36-49; John 20.19-23).

The stories are testimonies of faith in the risen Christ, not arguments or evidence to prove the resurrection. Paul's list of resurrection appearances in 1 Corinthians 15.3-8, written in the early 50s but originating some years before, is as near as we can get to the historical bedrock. That bedrock should probably also include the story of an early visit by a few female followers of Jesus to the tomb where he had been buried (e.g. Mark 16.1-8). Some of the names in that story vary, but it is unlikely that the early church would have invented a story featuring women, since women were often regarded as unreliable witnesses.

So, I am asking

- readers who are sceptical about the resurrection at least to consider that there was a mysterious 'something' after the crucifixion which is not easily explained away,

- Christian readers to look at the resurrection with fresh eyes; like the existence of God, it can't be proved — otherwise, their faith would not be faith.

But our subject is about much more than what happened. It is about what the resurrection, if true, actually meant.

The Resurrection's Meaning

There are three big themes in the resurrection stories themselves.

First, the resurrection marked the beginning of a worldwide mission (Matthew 28.16-20). Jesus, in his life, anticipated the God who would cross all boundaries. Now his disciples begin to do so.

Second, the resurrection communicated forgiveness. The enigmatic ending of Mark's Gospel seems to mean that Jesus forgave the disciples who had denied and abandoned him; he kept his promise to them, even though they had not kept their promise to him (14.28; 16.7). Two other Gospels recognize that forgiveness of sins was central to future Christian proclamation and mission (Luke 24.47; John 20.23). This will concern us again in the next chapter. 'Forgiveness' (Greek *aphesis*) has a wider meaning in the New Testament than in contemporary English; it also means liberation or release from heavy burdens (as in Luke 4.18).

Third, the first Christians became convinced that the death and resurrection of Jesus fulfilled the scriptures. If we ask 'Which ones?', the New Testament answer is 'All of them' (see e.g. Luke 24.27, 44, as well as

1 Corinthians 15.3-8). With hindsight, the early church combed through 'the Old Testament' (as Christians were eventually to call the scriptures), and found many references there to Christ. Some references may seem to us more convincing than others. The fundamental point was this: the crucified and risen Messiah Jesus was now seen to be *the* representative of the God of the Scriptures, and the endpoint to which they pointed.

In a remarkably short time, they were even saying that Jesus *was* that God. (On this, see Chapters 6 and 7.)

The Resurrection and God

I have called the resurrection 'mysterious', not because nothing can be proved, but because, according to the New Testament, it is about God. If God left his son to rot in the grave, cursed by the religious, mocked by the irreligious, then the fate of Jesus puts a giant question-mark against everything he stood for, including all that he had ever said about God. The resurrection is about God as well as about Jesus, because it amounts to God's vindication of Jesus. If true, it could mean that Jesus, in what he said and did about God's kingdom, had been right. The kingdom was here to stay; even the death of Jesus had not stopped the kingdom in its tracks.

So the first disciples drew the conclusion that God had been there in the darkness of crucifixion and death after all. That is why this most question-begging event — the crucifixion of 'the Son of God' — becomes central to the Christian understanding of God. The kingdom, the power and the glory of God come to be seen quite differently through the prism of the cross and resurrection of Jesus. God, from now on, may be called — as in St Paul's letters — 'the God and Father of our Lord Jesus Christ'.

St Paul may have been one of the first followers of Jesus to see the 'game-changing' significance of the cross and resurrection, as in

> ...God's foolishness is wiser than human wisdom, and God's weakness (i.e. in the cross) is stronger than human strength (1 Corinthians 1.25).

So, the resurrection of Jesus wasn't and isn't just about life after death, though that is part of its significance. It is God's vindication of Jesus — God's 'Yes' to Jesus' life, teaching and even his death. This belief in the God who raised Jesus from death, together with the belief that this same God is the Creator of all things, are the twin pillars on which the Christian understanding of God rests.

The rest of this chapter will look at the life, death and teaching of Jesus in the light of the resurrection, which is, above all, about the reality and nature of God.

2. The Strange Things Jesus Said about God

Jesus said a lot about God — more than appears in most English translations of the New Testament Gospels.[1] He spoke in a Jewish way, as you would expect a Jew to speak. But what he said and how he said it was anything but predictable. That was true of what he did as well. He wasn't exactly the 'long-expected' Messiah (as a well-known Advent hymn has it) at all. If he really was the Messiah, he was a surprising, unexpected one.

Jesus brought no new information about God, telling people things about God they didn't know before (though many may have forgotten, or not been listening). Instead, Jesus announced that something — inseparable from himself — was happening. This is why two key questions in the Gospels are 'Who gave you this authority?' and 'Should we believe him?' Eventually, a new experience and understanding of God would emerge from what Jesus said and did — though not in his lifetime.

A Strange 'Kingdom'

Jesus' first words in the Gospels of Mark and Matthew read like a summary:

> The time is fulfilled; the kingdom of God is at hand. Repent and believe the Gospel (Mark 1.15; compare Matthew 4.17).

What was this 'kingdom'? 'Kingdom' is an old-fashioned word these days; we have more presidents than kings or queens, more republics than monarchies. But it's not easy to explain the teaching of Jesus about God without the word. The Jewish expression 'kingdom of God', rare in the Old Testament, but more common in later Jewish writings, does not refer to a place; it is a metaphor or symbol for God's actual reign. That raises all sorts of questions: what is this 'kingdom'; where is it, and how do you become part of it?

God's kingdom or rule raises a lot of other questions for us — as it had done in Old Testament times. Israel believed God was king — even king of the whole world. (See, for example, Psalms 96–99). But that was far from obvious. How can God be king in a world like this? Why does he allow wars and famines to happen? The list of queries could go on.

Writers of both Old and New Testaments recognized that the world at present is not the world as God wants it to be, and that God intends to lead it to the peace and harmony which are its proper destiny. But first we must see what Jesus said about God's rule, and then those actions of his which, in modern jargon, we might call 'demos' of that kingdom.

Stories about God's Kingdom

Leading characters in the parables which Jesus taught are a good clue. A king forgives a slave a debt of 'ten thousand talents' (Matthew 18.24), a truly absurd amount, since one talent alone was worth more than fifteen years' wages of a labourer.[2] Again, a man leaves for another country and gives huge sums of money to his servants (Matthew 25.14-30). (I will come back to the difficult conclusion of this story later.)

There is more of this 'world upside down' behaviour in the parables. An employer's pay structure is what would be called then and now economic madness: employees who had worked one hour are paid the same as those who had worked all day (Matthew 20.1-16). A farmer sows seed with careless profligacy (e.g. Mark 4.3-8). The patriarchal head of a family runs to meet his wayward son and forgives him in a way which went quite against the stiff, social norms of the day (Luke 15.11-32). To make things worse, contrary to some Christian versions of this story, the father in the story embraces the son *before*, not after, the son expresses his penitence (vv.20-21).

If these stories are about God and the way God 'rules' his world — and the prefaces to the stories, such as Matthew 18.23 and 20.1 suggest they are — then these little cameos portray an extraordinarily generous or recklessly extravagant God. We shall need to test this first impression against other evidence in the Gospels. But it might explain why, in another parable of Jesus, the most unlikely people are invited to the banquet of the Kingdom (Luke 14.15-24).

Other parables provide an image — usually a quite unexpected, even shocking one — of the rule of God. Contrary to expectations, the kingdom is hidden, insignificant and small, like a mustard seed — but it won't always be like that (e.g. Matthew 13.31-32). It works like leaven in a loaf (Luke 13.20-21). Intriguingly, leaven was a loaded image — a symbol of impurity, suggesting that there is something subversive about God's rule.

The kingdom is like seed growing secretly. There is a limit to what a farmer can do to make it grow; its growth won't slow down if he goes to sleep; it won't speed up if he stays up to watch it (Mark 4.26-29).

So, the parables of Jesus, especially their leading characters and images, are an important part of the Bible's teaching about God. There are other parables, but these, I believe, help to give us an overview.

Before we come to other teaching of Jesus, it's worth noting that his teaching and actions go together: each interprets the other. For example, the turning of water into wine reads like a parable of the kingdom: 120 gallons of wine at one wedding! (John 2.1-11). But such a super-abundance of wine was promised for the coming new age (Isaiah 25.6; Joel 3.18).

The Beatitudes and the Lord's Prayer

Other teaching of Jesus in the Gospels fills out the picture. The so-called 'beatitudes' pronounce 'blessed' those people who reflect the character of God — the gentle, the merciful, the peace-maker (e.g. Matthew 5.1-11). This confirms what the Bible consistently holds together: the relationship of humans with God can't be separated from their relations with their 'neighbour'.

For this reason it may be misleading to translate one verse as saying that this 'kingdom' is 'within you' (Luke 17.20). The Kingdom is also 'amongst you' (another possible translation). Spirituality, after all, can be phoney; the quality of human relationships are the acid test of whether it's genuine.

What of other teaching of Jesus? The only prayer which Jesus is on record as teaching his followers begins 'Our Father'. It was unusually short and simple — its shorter version especially so (Luke 11.2-4; compare Matthew 6.9-13). Most if not all of it has parallels in Jewish prayers of the time. But after Jesus' own lifetime some of its petitions would have had a new significance. 'Your Kingdom come' would be understood in the light of Jesus' teaching and demonstrations of the kingdom, whilst the prayer for 'daily bread' recalled the mysterious feeding of the 5,000, as well as the Old Testament story of daily bread or 'manna' (Exodus 16).

As for the word 'father', it was an image for God well-known in Old Testament times and later. Jesus did not invent it. But embedded in three places in the New Testament (all of it written originally in Greek), is the Aramaic word *Abba*, followed by the Greek word 'father' (Mark 14.36; Romans 8.15; Galatians 4.4). It was almost certainly remembered as a word Jesus used. It wasn't unique to him and it wasn't the equivalent of the English 'daddy', as if it were a word used only by children. But it was still a word of intimacy and warmth, and the word 'father' as a word for God was to become especially associated with Jesus, especially — as I noted earlier — after the crucifixion and resurrection. (But it doesn't make God masculine. See my earlier reference to the Christian 'apophatic' tradition in the Introduction, section 3, 'God and gods'.)

But now we must turn to some of the more cryptic and difficult teaching of Jesus.

'Hidden' References to God

I said earlier that Jesus said more about God than first appears. A good example comes from the Sermon on the Mount:

> Do not judge others, so that you may not be judged (Matthew 7.1).

This is an example of what scholars sometimes call 'the divine passive':[3] 'that you may not be judged' means 'that God may not judge you'.

There are more examples in the Gospels of this oblique way of referring to God, as in Mark's Gospel:

> ...the measure you give will be the measure you get, and still more will be given you (Mark 4.24; compare Matthew 7.2 and Luke 6.38).

Is that a promise or a threat? It is both, as the following verse shows:

> For to those who have, more will be given; and from those who have nothing, even what they have will be taken away.

This is a good example in Jesus' teaching of what Jewish scholars call 'measure for measure': generosity begets generosity, forgiveness generates more forgiveness, 'having' leads to more having. But the converse is true as well: the person who shrivels up in fear and self-centredness will only shrivel up more — unless a miracle of grace occurs.

The threat is realized in the sad case of the third servant in the parable of the talents who buries his 'talent' — the equivalent of more than 15 years' wages — in a hole in the ground (Matthew 25.18). But what are we to make of that servant's estimate of his employer's character, if, as seems likely, the employer represents God:

> Master, I knew that you were a harsh man, reaping where you did not sow... (v.24)?

Most translations make the problem worse, since the master seems to agree with his servant's assessment of his character: yes, he *is* a hard man! But our oldest New Testament manuscripts don't have punctuation marks, so the master's words could well have been a sad question: in effect, 'Is that what you think of me?' In other words, the third servant fails to see how generous his master has been.

Other sayings of Jesus refer to a future reckoning which will bring its surprises:

> All who exalt themselves will be humbled, and all who humble themselves will be exalted (Matthew 23.13 — see also Luke 14.11 and 18.14).

Yet other divine passives point to God's generosity:

> Ask and *it will be given* to you,
>
> Seek and you will find,
>
> Knock and the door *will be opened* to you (Matthew 7.7, Luke 11.9).

This brings us back to an earlier theme: in the teaching of Jesus the generosity and forgiveness of God exceed people's wildest dreams. Does this contradict what the Old Testament says about God? No, it doesn't. There are memorable passages about the forgiveness of God, such as Psalms 103.8-12, 107.10-22, Isaiah 54.7-10 and Jeremiah 31.31-34, with its promise of a new covenant. God is portrayed there, too, as a shepherd looking for his lost sheep (Ezekiel 34.11-16; Luke 15.3-7). God will even answer his people's prayers before they've spoken them (Isaiah 65.24a; compare Matthew 6.8).

But now, as the Gospels keep saying, there is something new: a man speaking and acting for God with unprecedented authority, a man whose deepest identity didn't emerge fully until after his death.

In summary, what Jesus said about God's kingdom and about God as 'father' might be considered his answer to a crucial question about God: how does God 'exercise' his authority and power as Creator in his world?

But the Gospels have more to say about this, as we shall see.

Sayings about Eternal Punishment

Not all that Jesus said about God is as attractive as the themes I have just outlined, and I turn now to the many sayings in the Gospels which appear to threaten eternal punishment from God.

These days we tend to believe that punishment should not just punish, but reform the wrongdoer. Punishments must still deter, and some crimes are so heinous, and the offender so dangerous, that only a life sentence will do. But, these cases apart, we are inclined to think that most people deserve a second chance, especially if they've had a rotten start in life. So, what are we to make of Gospel sayings which seem to speak of eternal punishment?

There are two recurring themes: the threat of 'fire', and the prospect of 'weeping and gnashing of teeth'. The image of fire occurs in Mark:

If your hand causes you to stumble, cut it off; it is better for you to

enter life maimed than to have two hands and to go to hell, to the

unquenchable fire (9.43).[4]

Jesus can't have meant his teaching here to be taken literally — seriously, yes, literally, no. For one thing, the Hebrew Scriptures forbade mutilation. Similarly, as often in the Bible, the 'fire' here must be a symbol of destruction. So, this is a dire warning, to be taken seriously, yet interpreted in the light of the New Testament as a whole. I return to this question shortly.

As for 'weeping and gnashing of teeth', this occurs with one exception in Matthew's Gospel (Matthew 8.12; 13.42, 50; 22.13; 24.51; 25.30 — otherwise only Luke 13.28). So, it's possible that Matthew himself has added some of these references. But it would be wishful thinking to imagine that none at all goes back to Jesus.

As we struggle to understand this difficult language in the Gospels, one more detail in Matthew's Gospel may help a little. In the 'parable' of the sheep and the goats (25.31-46), 'the kingdom' (v.34) has been prepared for the righteous, whereas the 'eternal punishment' (v.46) has been prepared for 'the devil and his angels'; there is no reference here to humans. That's a significant difference in wording, suggesting that there is a 'bias' in the eternal purpose of the Creator towards human wellbeing — not destruction. But the searching challenge of this parable remains.

Making Sense of It

How is this darker side of Jesus' teaching to be related to the earlier themes of God's generosity and forgiveness? It is all too easy to think of God as an indulgent parent or as a stern, unbending judge. Both pictures can reflect our own preferences, including, sometimes, what we think should happen to people of whom we strongly disapprove.

We shall need to look once more at the biblical theme of God's judgement and 'punishments' (Chapter 7). But here we note the conclusion of a New Testament scholar who has made a more detailed study of these difficult themes than most. Stephen Travis concludes that, although biblical language about punishment sometimes sounds retributive, it is not so. 'Judgement is not punishment imposed "from outside" by God...it is the inevitable consequence of a person's refusal to enter into relationship with God... Love, by its very nature cannot force itself upon people'[5] — to which we might add: 'because love cannot violate the dignity and autonomy of another without being untrue to its very nature'.

The reply which Jesus gives to the question from John the Baptist, (literally) 'Are you the Coming One?', provides an apt conclusion to this section:

> Go and tell John what you have seen and heard: the blind receive their sight, the lame walk, the lepers are cleansed, the deaf hear, the dead are raised, the poor have good news brought to them. And blessed is anyone who takes no offence at me (Luke 7.22-23; see also Matthew 11.4).

This brings us, almost, to the heart of the Bible's understanding of God, and God's 'programme' for creation. But who could possibly take 'offence' at Jesus? To that question we now turn.

3. Not a God for Religious People

The life and teaching of Jesus begged a lot of questions. Who gave him the authority to speak and act like he did? *What* he did was undeniable. But where did his power come from? Questions like these were scattered like confetti across Galilee, where, it seems, Jesus spent the three years (by traditional reckoning) which preceded his death.

But it wasn't just what Jesus said or implied by his actions about God's rule which raised eyebrows. What he did often sent those eyebrows, if that were possible, even higher. He had meals with 'sinners', a word which referred to the kind of people whose job or lifestyle made them religiously or morally suspect (to put it mildly). Men who were agents of the hated occupying power of Rome were 'sinners' (e.g. Mark 2.14; Luke 15.1; 19.2). So were women who were prostitutes or had committed adultery (Luke 7.36-50; John 8.1-11).

Jesus in Bad Company

The kind of people he healed also made a statement about God's mysterious, ground-breaking kingdom — and God's holiness. For example, a leper who had to be isolated (e.g. Mark 1.39-45, and the prohibitions in Leviticus 13 and 14), or a demented individual living in a cemetery in a region deemed to be unclean (e.g. Mark 5.1-20) did not make Jesus 'unclean'. The opposite happened. Stories like these imply that something new is being said about the holiness of God.

Other stories involving Jesus show him healing people who had been marginalized not only because of their perceived impurities, but because of their disabilities or low economic status: a woman with a haemorrhage, a blind beggar, a widow whose son had died (e.g. Mark 5.25-34; 10.46-52; Luke 7.11-17). What made matters worse in the eyes of some religious people was the fact that Jesus performed some of these healings on the sabbath. The religious said they did not constitute urgent work; Jesus took the view that the sabbath was a good day for celebrating and anticipating the Kingdom of God (e.g. Luke 13.11-17; John 9).

Jesus also linked his exorcisms with the kingdom (Luke 11.20; Matthew 12.28). Most of his healing miracles, demonstrating the 'bias' of Israel's God to the poor, the least and the marginalized, illustrated what he was saying about God's Kingdom: the most unlikely people are welcome.

God and the Destiny of Jesus

A similar trail of questions marked the route Jesus took to Jerusalem. The residents of a Samaritan village refused him hospitality, and two of his disciples wanted to know why he didn't invoke fire from heaven as a punishment (Luke 9.51-56). He invited himself to the home of Jericho's most notorious resident, and people grumbled 'Why?' (Luke 19.1-10). He entered Jerusalem in some style — though not military style — and people asked questions (e.g. Mark 11.1-11).

Where was all this leading? The short answer was 'Jerusalem'. But what did that mean? Three of the four Gospels credit Jesus with predicting three times, like the tolling of a bell, his death and resurrection from death (e.g. Mark 8.31; 9.31; 10.33-34). In the story of Jesus, the cross casts a long shadow.

In these predictions God isn't explicitly mentioned. But two words are especially important. The first is the word 'must': 'the Son of Man' (the cryptic expression by which Jesus seems to have referred to himself) 'must' suffer. Here the word 'must' means 'it is part of God's purpose'. That is extraordinary enough, given what lay ahead of Jesus.

The other mysterious word (one word in the Greek) is 'hand over': the Son of Man 'will be handed over' to suffering and death. But who will hand Jesus over? The Gospels give two obvious answers to that question. Judas, one of his disciples, will (e.g. Matthew 26.14-16), and so will 'the chief priests and scribes' (Mark 10.34). But in this language there is more than a hint that God is involved too: as St Paul says:

He was handed over for our transgressions (Romans 4.23).

So, God and Judas (plus the Jewish leaders) hand Jesus over. That doesn't mean that Judas was a mere puppet on a divine string, though some of the Gospels' language might suggest that (Matthew 27.3-10; Acts 1.16-20; John 17.12).

The Old Testament background of the word 'hand over' is important. Psalmists and prophets alike asserted their conviction that God had handed over the people of Israel to experience the consequence of their sins (Psalm 106.41; Ezekiel 16.27). Rather than 'God handed them over', we might prefer to say, 'God *did not intervene*'; he let events run their course.

So, in the Gospels, as the death of Jesus loomed inexorably nearer, God did not intervene. Yet, in the view of the Gospel writers — or, to put it another way, in the light of the resurrection — Jesus was the innocent party; everyone else, including even his disciples, were the guilty ones.

So where, in the end, was God?

The disciples may have hoped right to the end that God would intervene. Some of their contemporaries expected that the Messiah, when he came, would come from the Mount of Olives. Those who mocked the tortured figure hanging from his cross clearly thought that divine intervention was the acid test of whether this man was a blasphemer or a man of God:

> …If you are the Son of God, come down from the cross (Matthew 27.39; compare v.43).

Even in Jesus' dying moments the possibility of a divine last-minute rescue was mooted:

> Wait, let us see whether Elijah will come to save him (v.49; compare Mark 15.36).

It is the response to what reads like Jesus' own cry of despair:

> My God, my God, why have you forsaken me? (Matthew 27.46; Mark 15.34).

So, God handed over 'the Son of Man'; *he did not intervene.* This 'silence' of God raised the biggest question of all about the God whom Jesus purported to speak for and represent. Is this tortured figure on the cross really 'the Son of God'? And, if so, what does God's silence mean?

According to the New Testament, only the sequel to the crucifixion answered those questions, and, in so doing, both confirmed and transformed the Old Testament understanding of God, as I hope to show more fully in the next chapters.

4. The Virgin Birth: Jesus — Human and Divine?

Finally, in this chapter, we turn to what is popularly called 'the Virgin Birth'. This is the story of how Mary the mother of Jesus became pregnant before she and Joseph, her betrothed husband, had had sexual intercourse (Matthew 1.18-25; Luke 1.26-38). We ask, first, whether it's true, and, second, what are the implications for our understanding of God.

Is the Virgin Birth True?

'Christmas will never be the same again', said the man mournfully, when I suggested that the Christmas stories of shepherds and wise men in the Gospels of Luke and Matthew are probably imaginative portrayals rather than historical accounts. But does that assessment, shared by many though not all New Testament scholars, include the virgin birth?

The origin of this story is not easy to explain. It's not like pagan stories of, say, a Greek god getting a girl pregnant. The early Christians may have derived the idea from a verse in the Old Testament: 'a virgin shall conceive' (Isaiah 7.14). But that prophecy in Isaiah is quite obscure; the prophet certainly wasn't predicting a virgin birth. For one thing, the

Hebrew word used here (*almah*) can, but doesn't necessarily, mean 'virgin'. The Greek version of Isaiah 7.14, called the Septuagint, *does* have a word — *parthenos* — which means 'virgin'. But it's unlikely that Greek-speaking Christians 'invented' this story on the basis of their Greek scriptures.

So where did the story come from? Could it possibly have been true? There was a later Jewish tradition that Mary became pregnant by a Roman soldier, and modern writers have argued that Jesus was illegitimate, partly on the basis of John 8.41, where the crowd's words to Jesus could be paraphrased '*We* (emphatic) are not illegitimate'.

More relevant was the way in which peoples of the ancient world developed stories about the remarkable births of distinguished men: patriarchs, kings, emperors. In Jewish traditions that includes stories about the birth of Moses, especially. So, these parallels may have influenced the early Christians.

More importantly, I don't think these speculations have much, if any, bearing on our subject here. The Virgin Birth features rarely in the New Testament. It's in two of the four Gospels (Matthew 1.18-25; Luke 1.26-38), and nowhere else. Some verses in Paul suggest a normal birth (Galatians 4.4; Romans 1.3), whilst John's Gospel speaks of a divine birth for all Christians (John 1.12-13).

What is more, no New Testament writer argues that Jesus 'must have been' born of a virgin in order to be perfect, sinless and divine. That was a later, mistaken argument. Not even Matthew argues that Jesus was the Son of God *because* he was born of a virgin. So, we are left with one verse, and only one, in the entire New Testament:

The angel said to her (*sc.* Mary): 'the Holy Spirit will come upon you… *therefore* the holy one who is to be born will be called the Son of God' (Luke 1.35).

Even this doesn't 'prove' the Virgin Birth. Without access to Luke's mind, we can't be sure whether he thought the words he was writing precluded human fatherhood or not. One more verse in Luke is relevant. In his version of the genealogy of Jesus, he writes that Joseph *'was thought'* to be Jesus' father. But even that is ambiguous.

A recent discussion concludes like this:

> If it is possible to talk of a consensus on such a controversial matter, it is probably this: the historical evidence for a virginal conception is very thin, but none of the alternative theories are especially convincing.[6]

I suggest that the Virgin Birth is marginal to our enquiry. Can a theological belief be based on a biological fact, anyway, if such it was? God is more important than Joseph for our understanding of Jesus' identity, and the baby — vulnerable and tiny as he was — more important than Mary for understanding the character of God.

Towards Understanding the Virgin Birth

In that same passage in Luke's Gospel, the angel Gabriel calls Mary *'kecharitomene'*: literally, 'graced' or 'favoured' (from the Greek *charis*, meaning 'grace'). This quality — God's undeserved love and favour — is *the* hallmark, according to large swathes of the New Testament, of what God does in the world (e.g. John 1.14; 2 Corinthians 8.9; 1 Timothy 1.2).

This undeserved love was first evidenced in God's 'election' of Israel (Deuteronomy 7.7-8).

The word 'grace' these days usually refers to physical grace — of a dancer, for example — or to a prayer said before a meal. But in the Bible grace is that mysterious, extraordinarily generous power of God which transforms human lives without overriding human freedom. We sometimes see such grace in human life — though not enough (yet) to change the world.

It is along these lines that 'the virgin birth' must be understood. From the first moment of conception, the life of Jesus was the work of God's grace. He did not later qualify for, or earn, the title 'son of God'. That was his from birth — or even before. (See, for example, 2 Corinthians 8.9 and Philippians 2.6.) This, I suggest, is a more helpful approach than getting bogged down in discussions about Jesus' parental DNA.

Clearly, the title 'Son of God', like all language about God, can't be understood literally. It had various meanings in Jesus' day: in the Jewish world, 'king of Israel' (see Psalm 2.7), an angel (Job 38.7), a holy man (Ecclesiasticus 4.10); in the wider Graeco-Roman a world, a hero or an emperor was often called a Son of God.

5. Summary

The resurrection cast the retrospective light of God over all that had gone before, confirming the presence and blessing of God on Jesus' life teaching, and even his death.

Jesus spoke and acted for an astonishingly generous and disturbing God whose 'kingdom' was near — accessible even to, or especially for, the last, the least and the lowest. In addressing God, Jesus taught his followers to use an intimate parental image: 'Father'.

Jesus disturbed religious people more than most, not only by what he said, but by the company he kept. Eventually he paid for that with his life.

All this is why Jesus was to become central to the Christian understanding of God. Matthew's Gospel anticipates this new understanding: Jesus is 'Immanuel... God with us' (Matthew 1.23; Isaiah 7.14), and so the risen Jesus speaks like God: '...I am with you always...' (Matthew 28.20).

But the understanding of God reflected in later Christian creeds does not obviously flow from the first three Gospels. Many have questioned later developments, such as the doctrine of the Trinity. So, in the next two chapters we turn to two New Testament writers who were to be especially influential in the decades and centuries which followed.

6. Looking Ahead

This chapter has focussed on the Gospels of Matthew, Mark and Luke. But the revolutionary implications of Jesus, vindicated (in the Christian view), in the resurrection, needed to be 'unpacked' a great deal more. Paul's letters, all written before those Gospels, begin from this new perspective: 'Grace and peace to you from God our Father *and* the Lord Jesus Christ' (e.g. Romans 1.7). In these letters, written to churches comprised mostly if not entirely of Gentiles, the cross and resurrection are the 'epicentre' of Paul's thinking, and we shall explore this further in the next chapter.

The world — including, often, the Church — still resists, or struggles to grasp the significance of a crucifixion for our understanding of God. Crucifixion and resurrection in the New Testament belong together — two sides of the same coin — and together they represent the way in which God as God really is relates to his creation: crucified yet undefeated, suffering yet mysteriously victorious, self-effacing and selfless, yet still the creative power which rolls through all things, still the all-pervasive breath sustaining the whole universe, and always a 'You' for whom the image of father or mother would seem to be the closest we can get.

The Gospel of John, discussed in Chapter 7, was almost certainly completed later than both Paul's letters and the other Gospels. 'John' seems to be making more explicit what is implied in Matthew, Mark and Luke. In John we take a step nearer later Church doctrines: the 'divinity' of Jesus and the 'Holy Trinity' — i.e. God as 'Father, Son and Holy Spirit'.

If this line of thought is correct, the germ of these later doctrines is already there in the New Testament. In fact, the doctrine of the Trinity might be thought of as a more developed expression, in the light of Jesus, of the biblical faith in an outgoing Creator and a Reality who is a 'You' rather than an 'It'. (On this, see also the end of Chapter 7.)

'Outgoing' is a central theme in this story of God. The Church's mission to the Gentiles dominates much of the New Testament. Think of Jesus befriending Zaccheus, godfather of swindlers and compromised people everywhere (Luke 19.1-10), and make it global. That's what had begun to happen.

* * *

Three Questions for Reflection and Discussion

1 Try looking at the Gospels 'backwards': what are the implications for Christian faith and life of regarding the resurrection as God's 'Yes' to Jesus?

2 The scribes and Pharisees were not religious bigots (few people are), but human beings who were trying to live a moral life (as many — perhaps most — people do). But judging other people seems to be part and parcel of this moral approach to life. Was this why Jesus was crucified?

3 'Never was Jesus more truly God than when he felt himself forsaken by God' (William Temple). What do you think Temple's words mean? Do you agree?

Going Deeper: Further Reading

John Dickson, *Jesus: A Short Life. The Historical Evidence* (Lion, 2012).

James D.G. Dunn, *Did the First Christians Worship Jesus? The New Testament Evidence* (SPCK, 2010).

Neil Richardson, *God in the New Testament* (Epworth/SCM, 1999).

Endnotes

1   See the later discussion about the 'divine passive', a distinctively Jewish way of referring to God without mentioning God.

2   So the NRSV. Other modern translations don't quite convey just how fantastic the sums of money were here.

3   This 'divine passive' may have come originally from the royal court: it was thought presumptuous to address or even refer directly to the king; one should do so indirectly.

4   It is difficult to be sure how many such references there are in this section of Mark, because our manuscripts vary. But there is a similar saying at Matthew 18.8.

5   Stephen H. Travis, *Christ and the Judgement of God: The Limits of Divine Retribution in New Testament Thought* (Paternoster/Hendrickson, 2009), p.326.

6   Steve Moyise, *Was the Birth of Jesus according to Scripture?* (SPCK, 2013), p.101.

6

Paul:
The God Who Crossed
Boundaries

In a family...love and 'grace' — i.e. forgiveness are the
bottom line, the prevailing 'law'.

St Paul has had a bad press in many quarters. Quite apart from what he is supposed to have said about women and about homosexuality (about which more later), he has been variously portrayed as guilt-ridden, authoritarian, and intolerant. It's not easy to get a clear picture of this man, especially as his letters[1] are often cryptic and don't tell us very much about his actual life.

But what does he teach about God? Does it bear any relation to what Jesus taught — about the Kingdom of God, for example? And what effect on his understanding of God did his famous Damascus Road conversion have? Surprisingly, this question hasn't often been asked.

So, in this chapter we ask

* how Paul's conversion affected his inherited faith in God and his attitude to Gentiles,

- what God had to do with the death of Jesus, and what Paul meant by calling Jesus 'Lord',

- what Paul has to say about sin, the place of women, homo-sexuality and the wrath of God,

- how his understanding of God and church are connected.

1. God on the Damascus Road

The twentieth-century Christian writer and activist Beyers Naudé had an experience not unlike Paul's, although for him the change was more gradual. Naudé was a South African who grew up in a strongly nationalist Afrikaner family. He became a leading light in the Dutch Reformed Church, subscribing to the racial policies of the apartheid system of the time, and the theology which underwrote it. But he came to question the faith he had inherited. He founded the ecumenical Christian Institute which became a vocal opponent of apartheid until it was outlawed. Naudé himself was served with banning orders, and severely restricted in his travel for many years. Spiritually, however, he had travelled a long way, crossing the deep racial divide which scarred the South Africa of his day.

How Paul Changed

Paul made a similar journey. He never calls himself a 'Christian'.[2] In fact, he never uses the word 'Christian', but from being what we would now call 'a practising Jew', a devout Pharisee (Philippians 3.5), he became Christ's apostle to the Gentiles, mixing freely with people he had previously thought impure or godless or both. His Damascus Road experience was the immediate cause of this extraordinary U-turn. What happened, and how did his view of God change?

In Luke's version of that event in the Acts of the Apostles there is a blinding light, a voice from heaven ('I am Jesus whom you are persecuting', e.g. Acts 9.5), and a commission to take the gospel to the Gentiles.[3] Paul's 'take' on what happened is different: he believed he had seen the risen Jesus, just as Peter and the other apostles had (1 Corinthians 9.1; 15.3-8). Whatever happened, it changed forever Paul's understanding of God. (Here I differ from those scholars who think that his new belief in Jesus simply 'slotted in' to his inherited Jewish beliefs about God.)

We should forget, by the way, the older Christian view of Paul as a guilt-ridden Pharisee until he met Christ. There is no New Testament evidence for this. It seems, instead, that his conversion cast a new light on his previous way of life, and especially on Gentiles and the new sect eventually called 'Christians' (Acts 11.26).

Paul had persecuted the early followers of Jesus out of his 'zeal' for God (Galatians 1.13-14). In his eyes they were God's enemies, perhaps because they didn't keep the law of Moses as strictly as he thought they should, or because — horror of horrors — they believed in a Messiah who had been crucified. But now Paul encountered the crucified Jesus in a vision on the Damascus Road. If that was for real, and Paul clearly believed it was, that could only mean that this crucified man had not, after all, been cursed or forsaken by God, despite what the law of Moses said (Deuteronomy 21.23; Galatians 3.13). He really was the Messiah of God — as the Christians claimed. It was all or nothing — a complete U-turn.

A New World

So, Paul's map of the world changed. No longer Jerusalem-centred, the world and its peoples were as much the object of God's love as Israel, its people and its land were. God is no longer simply 'our' God, but God of the Gentiles as well (Romans 3.29). Paul would have believed, of course, that God was God of all nations, as his Hebrew scriptures often asserted, but a Jerusalem- or Israel-centred perspective inevitably marginalized 'the Gentiles'. (A church-centred perspective today does the same: marginalizes the people Christian congregations unfortunately refer to sometimes as 'outsiders'.)

But there was an underlying reason why Paul's map of the world changed. Central to his new understanding of God was a belief that God had 'crossed boundaries' in a way which turned Paul's old world upside down. The righteousness of God had been revealed in — of all things — a crucifixion (Romans 3.21-26). As for God's holiness, this was a holiness which did not hold aloof from the deepest depths to which human life could sink. Paul hardly ever calls God or Jesus holy. But he clearly believed that the 'Holy Spirit' of God emerged in a new and powerful way out of the scandal of the cross and the mystery of the resurrection. What is more, this holy presence spread all over the unclean lands of the eastern Mediterranean, making even Gentiles holy. You might say there was a lot here for a converted Pharisee to think about.

God of Christ Crucified

The cross of the Christ (God's Messiah) was the crucible in which this new understanding of God was forged. Although what Paul wrote to the church at Corinth about 'God's foolishness and weakness' (1 Corinthians

1.25) has some faint parallels in Old Testament and Jewish sources, Paul the Pharisee could never have written words like these.

We have little idea how much Paul knew of the life and teaching of Jesus, since he rarely refers to either.[4] He once stayed a fortnight with Simon Peter ('Cephas', Galatians 1.18), but, as someone once remarked, they would hardly have spent a fortnight discussing the weather. It is likely that Paul came to believe that the death of Jesus summed up his life; Jesus died for his beliefs and for all that he had lived for. For instance, he had associated with 'dodgy' characters and unclean people ('sinners', lepers, women accused of adultery, among others). So, to end up crucified between two criminals was at least consistent. Again, he had healed people, and his followers came to believe that his death, in some mysterious way, healed the whole world (e.g. 2 Corinthians 5.19; Ephesians 2.14-16).

So, what emerged from Paul's conversion was an understanding and experience of God centred on the cross and resurrection of Jesus. In these events the power of God had transcended barriers which divided people both from each other and also from God. The resurrection of Christ offered the hope that the last boundary of all, death itself, would ultimately be defeated (1 Corinthians 15.55-57).

Now, the human race begins to re-group around a crucified God — or, in Paul's words, 'in Christ'. (I explore this further in the next section.) The cross of Christ was the place, according to Paul, where God found the human race; here the stories of God and humankind converged, constituting 'a new creation' (Galatians 6.15; 2 Corinthians 5.17). But this was not a case of stalactite and stalagmite growing towards each other and meeting in the middle. Paul insists that God took the initiative:

In Christ God was reconciling the world to himself... (2 Corinthians 5.19).

Old and New, God and Jesus

Did all this mean that Paul's view of God was now quite different? Not
quite. As a devout Jew, he would have believed in the love and grace of
the God about whom his scriptures spoke. But this new revelation, as the
saying goes, was 'something else'. So, now he interweaves words about
God and words about Jesus; a reference to one prompts a reference to
the other. The opening sentence of most of his letters says it all, as in
1 Corinthians 1.3:

> Grace and peace to from God our Father and the Lord Jesus
> Christ...

There is also an exuberance about Paul's language. A good example
occurs in his letter to the Romans. After enumerating the hardships and
deprivations he faced as an apostle of Christ, he concludes:

> ...in all these things we are more than conquerors through him who
> loved us. For I am convinced that neither death, nor life, nor angels,
> nor rulers, nor things present nor things to come, nor powers, nor
> height, nor depth, nor anything else in all creation, will be able to
> separate us from the love of God in Christ Jesus our Lord (Romans
> 8.37-39).

The reference here to Jesus is the key, as two rhetorical questions at the
start of this lyrical passage show:

If God is for us, who is against us? He who did not withhold his own Son, but gave him up for all of us, will he not with him also give us everything else? (Romans 8.31b-32).[5]

In the next section we shall look more closely at what Paul says about Jesus and how it relates to his understanding of God, and to Christian experience as expressed by Paul.

2. Jesus: In Our Place and in God's Place

Paul's language about God is strewn with references to Jesus or 'Christ'. But how did Paul see the relationship between God and Jesus — especially with reference to the crucifixion?

Did God Punish Jesus?

Unfortunately, Christian tradition has tended to think of the crucifixion of Jesus in legal terms. There was a penalty to pay, and Jesus, God's son, paid it. God's righteousness and justice had to be upheld, so Jesus suffered the punishment in place of us. God's love has to be balanced by his holiness, so he can't just let us off without someone paying the price.

All of this is simply bad theology. What is more, it is unbiblical. The language of relationship is more appropriate than legal or penal terms. Already in the Old Testament, people were beginning to see that 'the Holy One of Israel' was the One who came to the help of Israel. The righteousness of God consisted in God keeping his promises (whatever humankind did), especially his promise to save his people. And God's people, according to Paul, comprises potentially everyone.

So, Paul's language about God 'handing over' his Son does not mean God taking it out on Jesus, or Jesus being punished in place of us. What did matter to the apostle was that God and Jesus were 'hand in glove' in reconciling the world to God: the meaning of the frequent phrase 'Christ died for our sins'.

A Brief Aside on the Letter to the Hebrews

I mention Hebrews here only because Richard Dawkins[6] thinks it is guilty of the 'scapegoating' I've just mentioned: God punished Jesus. This is a misreading of Hebrews. The letter's introduction (1.1-4) provides the key:

> ...in these last days he (*sc.* God) has spoken to us by a Son... He is the reflection of God's glory and the exact imprint of God's very being...

The writer goes on to address 'the Son' as God (1.8). So, if Jesus in some way *is* God, 'scapegoating' doesn't arise. Jesus, in the argument of Hebrews, is both priest *and* sacrificial victim, but, crucially, as other New Testament writers claim or imply, he is God for us, God with us.

The Divine Exchange

This is where, according to Christian faith, the two stories of the Bible, the divine and the human, converge. God shared our human life, that we, in Christ, might share God's life. This is the 'divine exchange' about which one scholar in particular (Professor Morna Hooker of Cambridge), has written in recent years: God in Christ shared the life of humankind in order that humankind, through Christ, might share God's life.

Paul expresses this divine exchange in different ways, depending on what he's talking about, and to whom. (See Galatians 4.4-6, 2 Corinthians 8.9 and Romans 8.3-4 for three examples.) One expression of this exchange is especially startling:

> For our sake he (*sc.* God) made him (*sc.* Jesus) to be sin who knew no sin, so that in him we might become the righteousness of God (2 Corinthians 5.21).

This is Paul at his most radical and paradoxical: the crucified Jesus in the depths of human existence, indistinguishable from the rest of us.

Understanding what Paul means by 'Christ' and 'in Christ', and *where* this reality is, will help us appreciate what Paul is saying about God. In Paul's writings, 'Christ' has become a kind of 'surname' attached to the individual Jesus, the 'first' son of God (Romans 8.29; John's Gospel was later to call Jesus God's only-begotten son, John 3.16).

According to Paul, the divine and the human also meet in everyone 'in Christ' — that is, 'through Jesus Christ, our Lord'. That is humanity's secret, it is made in the image of God: 'Christ in you' (Colossians 1.27). So, there is a mysterious convergence between the human 'me' and 'Christ'. In Galatians 2.20a we read:

> I live — yet it is no longer 'I', but Christ who lives in me.

'Christ' is the human potentiality of every person, unlocked by 'God in Christ': the divine exchange.

Christ the Outreach of God

What has all this to do with Paul's understanding of God? Simply this, that in Paul's thinking and (we might guess) experience, 'Christ' is the outreach of God to the human world: God's 'righteousness' (e.g. Romans 1.17; 3.21-26), God's 'wisdom' (1 Corinthians 1.24, 30), God's 'son' (Galatians 2.20-21; Romans 8.31-32). That outreach reached its culminating point in the death of Jesus. It was as if there was no further to go, no lower point to sink to, no further battles to win — or lose.

As the dust begins to settle and the skies to clear in this post-crucifixion world, a new world begins to emerge (2 Corinthians 5.17). The 'rule-book' has been torn up (Colossians 2.14-15); this God is not (apparently) almighty, but powerless — not the victor, but the victim. At the same time, Paul had seen something deeper:

> ...God's weakness is stronger than human strength (1 Corinthians 1.25).

We might say that this God, who in retrospect came to be seen ('revealed') in the cross of Jesus, was the God who wrong-footed everyone. He certainly wrong-footed Paul on the road to Damascus. The enemies of God were not who he thought they were. In fact, God had no enemies at all.

The Friendship of God

Paul uses remarkably inclusive language about this divine outreach. It's accessible to everyone. (Paul's letters are peppered with the words 'every' and 'all'.) If we ask how, Paul's answer is simple. The life of God can be accessed through 'faith'. Faith seems to mean 'reaching out a hand to grasp God's hand, already stretched out in friendship to you.[7] That analogy suggests a human action, but it's a bit more mysterious than that. Faith is where the human and divine converge, and where does one begin and the other end? In Paul's thinking, you can't really tell, because 'the Holy Spirit' — God's 'breath' in every human being alive — makes this faith possible.

So, to do justice to Paul's understanding of God, we end up on the verge of 'Trinitarian' language: 'the grace of our Lord Jesus Christ, the love of God, and the fellowship of the Holy Spirit' (2 Corinthians 13.13). (On this, see also Chapter 7.)

But is Paul's God really as universal and inclusive as I have suggested here? There are darker themes in Paul to be explored, and they will be the subject of the next section.

Paul never calls Jesus 'God' in so many words. (Romans 9.5 might be the one exception.[8]) In fact, the New Testament as a whole is remarkably reticent about what the Church was later to call the divinity of Jesus. The title 'Christ' was the Greek equivalent of the Hebrew 'Messiah', a concept which would have meant little to Gentiles unfamiliar with the Jewish tradition. Instead, Paul constantly refers to Jesus as 'Lord': the 'Lord Jesus Christ'. (Messiah wasn't a divine title anyway; it didn't mean 'God', it meant 'anointed' — i.e. God's anointed.)

Jesus is 'Lord'

The word 'lord' had an important pedigree in Hebrew, in Aramaic (Jesus' own language) and in Greek. An ascending scale in its different meanings can be traced. It could be a term of respect from a stranger: the equivalent of our 'Sir'. It's the word the disciples often used to address Jesus as their leader. But after the resurrection it became a title by which the first Christians expressed their conviction that now Jesus was 'at the right hand of God' (Acts 2.34-36; see also Psalm 110.1, probably the most often quoted Old Testament verse in the New Testament).

'At God's right hand' seems to imply 'equal to, but not the same as God', and that is right — up to a point. Paul puts it very neatly:

> For us there is one God...and one Lord Jesus Christ... (1 Cor-inthians 8.6).

So far, Paul seems to be saying what Jesus says in the first three Gospels, whether in words original to him or attributed to him:

> All authority in heaven and on earth has been given to me... (Matthew 28.18).

(Here, as often in the New Testament, a passive verb — 'was given' means '*God* gave' — the 'divine passive' again [see Chapter 5, section 2, 'The Strange Things Jesus Said about God']).

But there is one more step to take in this ascending scale of meanings of the word 'lord'. Paul, in writing to Greek-speaking Gentiles, naturally quotes the Jewish Scriptures in Greek. In those Scriptures 'the Lord' occurs countless times as a title for God, replacing, or at least being read in place of, the sacred Hebrew name for God, 'Jehovah'. (In Hebrew, that name comprised four consonants: YHWH.)

'The Lord' is so common in the Old Testament that the reader soon starts to take it for granted: 'the Lord is God', 'God is the Lord', 'the Lord God' etc. So, when some of Paul's quotations from the scriptures refer to 'the Lord', as when he quotes the prophet Joel,

Everyone who calls on the name of the Lord will be saved (Romans 10.13),

who is 'the Lord' here? God or 'the Lord Jesus'? It could be either — or both. In Paul's mind, I suspect, it didn't really matter.

3. Some of Our Problems with Paul's God

I began this chapter by observing that Paul has had a bad press. Now we need to explore some of the reasons for this, relating them to what Paul, Christ's apostle to the Gentiles, had come to believe about the God who crossed boundaries.

Whether sin and sex were as prominent on Paul's agenda as people have supposed is doubtful. Sex certainly not; that was his churches' problem, not his. (See, e.g., 1 Thessalonians 4.3-8 and 1 Corinthians 7.) As for sin, Paul is widely misunderstood, and I turn to that first.

Paul and the Problem of Sin

The forgiveness of sin lies at the heart of Christian faith, or, at least, pretty close to it. That is clear from the New Testament. Jesus forgave sins, and commissioned his disciples to do the same (e.g. Mark 2.1-12; John 20.19-23). That was *the* message of the resurrection: a universal proclamation of the forgiveness of God (Luke 24.44-49).

In the modern era, God is often blamed for there being any sins to forgive in the first place. According to influential thinkers and writers such as Nietzsche and Freud, the Christian God is why there has been —

at least until recently — more guilt-feelings than ever amongst those who believe in God, or those who believe but perhaps subconsciously wish they didn't.

The Bible, and Paul in particular, seem to prove the truth of this charge. They have a lot to say about sin. A person's bad conscience and the guilt-feelings which go with it may be evidence that that person has 'committed a sin'. But they might not mean that at all. A person's conscience could be either sleepy or over-active (like an over-zealous filter on a computer).

What is 'Sin'?

In the Bible 'sin' is a personal, relational term: falling out of relationship with God and other people. Most if not all moral failures, in the biblical view, stem from these failed relationships. As always in the Bible, divine and human relations go together. If Israel's relationship with her God was askew, the poor in her midst were more likely to be oppressed, if Christians got a bit above themselves because they thought they were so spiritual, charity was likely to go out of the window (1 Corinthians 1.11-12 and chapter 13).

So why does Paul say so much about sin, especially in Romans, his longest letter? First, because humankind's relationship with God, individually and corporately, is supremely important. If there really is a 'Creator' whose 'breath' is the very life of the whole universe, then it must be.

Second, Paul, through his Damascus Road experience, had come to believe that God, through his Messiah or 'Son', had dealt with the relational problem which lay at the heart of human sinfulness: 'Christ died for our sins' (e.g. 1 Corinthians 15.3); '...in Christ God was reconciling the world to himself' (2 Corinthians 5.19). And here we come back to part of what's been called 'the new perspective' on Paul. The solution helped the apostle to identify the problem. To put it another way: with the advent of the light, it became easier to see the darkness for what it really was. (This is the imagery John's Gospel uses, especially John 1.1-14; 3.19-21.) God's outreach in Christ exposes *both* the world's distance from God *and* God's nearness to the world.

The Scandal of Paul's Preaching

Paul nowhere says 'God loves the sinner but hates the sin'. This has become an unhelpful, misleading cliché in some Christian circles. It's not that God can be said to approve of sin. If 'sin' is a relational term, how could the Creator be said to approve of a creation out of sync with its Origin? The figure we need to keep in mind in this discussion is the father in the parable Jesus told (Luke 15.11-32).

All of this suggests that the kind of preaching which aimed to make people feel sinful and guilty in order to 'convert' them is mistaken. The Bible gives a different picture. The prophet Isaiah realizes he is 'unclean' *after* his vision of God; that realization wasn't a condition for receiving the vision (Isaiah 6.1-5). Simon Peter confesses he is a sinner after he has become a disciple; it wasn't a condition for becoming one. In Christian tradition, saints are those people who become more, not less, aware of their shortcomings. But they also know they are still held in the love of God.

So, we need to look at Paul's extraordinary, even revolutionary teaching on sin afresh. It grew out of his experience of God. That teaching caused trouble in Paul's lifetime. We know that because Paul says so. People thought he was saying, 'Let's do evil that good may come' (Romans 3.6); 'let's go on sinning, because God will forgive us anyway' (Romans 6.1).

You might say, 'Paul had only himself to blame; just look at his argument in Romans!' To which Paul, I think, might reply, 'Don't blame me; I'm only the messenger! Blame Jesus, blame the gospel!'

So what did Paul say in Romans about sin?

The key passage is Romans 5.12-21. In most English translations, Paul's argument is tortuous. In the original Greek, his language is even more terse. Paul is comparing and contrasting Adam and Christ. To human sin God responds, not with thunderbolts, but with 'grace' — unmerited love. But even this was not a 'measure for measure' approach: a little grace, to see if it works, and if not... On the contrary,

> ...where sin was multiplied, grace immeasurably exceeded it (Romans 5.20b).

No wonder the only 'reasonable' response was the one Paul himself anticipates:

> So what are we going to say? Should we continue sinning so grace will multiply? (Romans 6.1; compare v.15).

What Really Changes People?

That rhetorical question of Paul's is a natural response from respectable, religious people worried (and rightly so) that the law, and the moral foundations of society are being undermined. Paul well knew, as we do, that without law there would be anarchy; society would collapse. You can't operate a judicial system on an undiluted diet of grace. And yet, far more criminals today might be rehabilitated if there were a better 'mix' in our criminal justice systems of both law and grace. (How, really, do you change people — i.e. help them to cross the boundaries they need to cross?)

We might add: in a family it's different. There, love and 'grace' — i.e. forgiveness — are the bottom line, the prevailing 'law'. Of course, there have to be 'rules' — especially until members of the family come of age (Galatians 3.23-25; 4.1-7) — for example, about whose turn it is to do the washing-up. But in a family it's love, not the law, which makes the world go round. In Jesus' parable of the prodigal son, the returning prodigal had no penalty to pay, no law to which he should bow, not even the justice of his father (whatever that was). This was — and is — the 'scandal' at the heart of what both Jesus and Paul taught about God, and why 'sin' was such a 'hot' topic in Paul's preaching and people's reaction to it.

At the heart of Paul's teaching about God and sin is a very simple insight — or perhaps I should say — experience: God gives what God requires. Paul hardly ever uses the word which occurs in the summary of Jesus' preaching: 'repent' (a much misunderstood word). But he uses language which points to the same transforming, liberating experience:

...be transformed by the renewal of your minds (Romans 12.2).

The 'renewal of minds' might suggest mind-teasers and crosswords for the over-70s, but Paul is not talking about some intellectual rejuvenation. He is pointing to the deeper transformation he himself had experienced, and which, we may presume, could never have been a D-I-Y job; only a power outside himself could accomplish it. (It can happen when two people fall in love).

Finally, and briefly, I turn in this section to three more of our problems with the apostle Paul, and what he said, or is thought to have said.

Paul, Marriage and Women

People have speculated about Paul's own sexuality: was he single, married, a widower or gay? Almost certainly single (1 Corinthians 7.1-7) — but more than that we can't say. What he says about sexual intercourse within marriage, however, is positive, and, by the standards of his day, notably mutual (v.3).

His references to women in his letters are a mixture of conventional (by the standards of the time) and radical. 'Wives obey your husbands' (Colossians 3.18, if written by Paul — see endnote 1) was commonplace; it's difficult to see what else Christian wives could have done in such a patriarchal culture, especially if their husband didn't share their faith. (On this, see 1 Peter 3.1-2.) On the other hand, in the final chapter of Romans he greets a remarkable number of women in positions of leadership (Romans 16). Elsewhere he says 'in Christ there is...neither male nor female' (Galatians 3.28). So, something new was stirring. Perhaps Paul's understanding of God was not as patriarchal as we have imagined.

Paul, Homosexuality and God

This is a subject too large and controversial to deal with adequately here. There are two or three references at most which are relevant: Romans 1.26-27, 1 Corinthians 6.9, and (if by Paul himself) 1 Timothy 1.10. Does

Paul's condemnation of the homosexual practices of his day (mostly, though not entirely, promiscuous and exploitative) still apply? His teaching needs to be understood in the light of its cultural and social background. For example, in the Graeco-Roman world a woman was regarded as a defective male, and that was why a male should not be the passive partner in a sexual relationship.

But this teaching also needs to be interpreted in the light of the revelation of God about which Paul presumes to speak. The implications of that revelation continue to be worked out, sometimes casting into sharp relief the more culture-specific commands of Paul such as 'Wives, obey your husbands'.

In Romans the apostle asks,

> Is God God of the Jews alone? Isn't he also God of the Gentiles?

answering his own question,

> Yes, God is God of the Gentiles as well (Romans 3.29).

In the light of the words he wrote, then, what might Paul write today? 'Is God of the Christians only? Is God not also God of Muslims, Buddhists...?' 'Is God God not only of heterosexual people, but also of people who are gay?'[9]

Paul, Predestination and Hell

Did Paul teach that God predestines some people to damnation and hell? This remains the view of some sincere, well-meaning Christian people. I think it rests on a serious misreading of the New Testament, and of Paul in particular.

The crucial passage is Romans 9–11. This long argument is one continuous whole, and it's important to see not just where Paul begins, but also where he ends up. All the preceding verses need to be interpreted in the light of the conclusion:

> For God has imprisoned all in disobedience so that he may be merciful to all (Romans 11.32).

The difficult first half of that verse seems to mean that even in our disobedience we can't get away from God. That's bad news if we want to stay disobedient — not that God is going to turn nasty, but because, in Paul's view, the darkness can only get darker (Romans 1.18-32 again).[10] But if we catch a glimpse of something better, and decide to make for home rather than stay in 'the far country' (to use the imagery of Jesus' story in Luke 15), then the presence of God in the far country is good news, not bad news.

The second half of this verse makes very clear the universal scope of God's generosity. Is this a wishful interpretation of Paul? An early interpreter of Paul certainly didn't think so:

> (God)…wants everyone to be saved and to come to the knowledge of the truth (1 Timothy 2.4).

If this interpretation of Paul is right, it follows that some translations of Romans 9.22 are more in keeping than others with Paul's overall thinking. The 'vessels of wrath' mentioned here cannot have been 'made for destruction', as the NRSV has it; but they are 'due for destruction' (so the REB). The whole point of Paul's argument — with Israel in his mind from start to finish — is that 'vessels of wrath' *may become* 'vessels of mercy'.

4. 'To the Church of God in Corinth'

Where does the Church fit into Paul's new world? A short but not necessarily convincing answer is this: the Church is a foretaste — an anticipation — of that new world. Out of the reconciliation — thanks to God's 'outreach' in Christ — of God and humankind, a re-grouping of the human race has begun to emerge — and that is the Church.

Not 'Church' as We Know It

To discover what Paul understands by 'church', we need to note his words carefully, use our historical imaginations — and also note what he doesn't say. Apart from a few features which have been part of the Church's DNA from the very beginning — faith in Jesus as 'Lord', observing 'the Lord's supper' (1 Corinthians 11.23-26) and the centrality of love, to mention just three — there were no church buildings and no structural organization to speak of, but plenty of visits, hospitality, a few letters (e.g. Acts 15.22 and Paul's own letters), and (at least) one collection (e.g. 1 Corinthians 16.1-3). To begin with, Christians weren't called 'Christians' at all, just 'disciples' or followers of 'the Way', according to Acts.

Paul talks about 'the saints' (literally, 'the holy ones'), which sounds very off-putting, until we realize that these words refer not to their moral achievements, but to their call by God. (That call, of course, brought its own moral imperatives.) Paul also has three other ways of referring to Christians and the Christian life, all of them important by-products of his new understanding of God. Christians are people who now, thanks to

God's friendship, are 'in Christ', who live 'in the Spirit', and whose ultimate allegiances are to 'the Lord Jesus', as the frequency of the phrase 'in the Lord' shows.

God's New Creation

But what was it all about, and where did God, as it were, fit in? To call the motley band of believers in Christ at Corinth 'the church of God' was remarkable in itself. They were Gentiles! And they lived in Corinth, a city which was not exactly a hotbed of morality. But, then, this was one of the outcrops of that outreach of God: 'Grace and peace to you from God our Father…' (1 Corinthians 1.3).

We note here how this fits into the Bible as a whole. If Jesus was where the Bible's two stories, divine and human, converge, then that is true also of those communities called 'the church of God' which were called to live 'in Christ', as befitted people who had been 'baptized into Christ' (e.g. Romans 6.3-8). They were part of God's 'new creation', transcending old boundaries (2 Corinthians 5.17; Galatians 6.15). They were founded by the one who was 'the image of God' (e.g. 2 Corinthians 4.4; cf. Genesis 1.27), but who, unlike other humans, reflected that image in all its glory. What was more, according to Paul, this 'latter day Adam', as Paul calls Jesus (1 Corinthians 15.45), had the generative power to restore that image in others.

From the beginning to the end of the Bible, human wellbeing and the glory of God are closely connected. Given that humankind is made in the image of God (Genesis 1.27), we would expect that to be so. The glory of God and the real glory of human beings are not opposed to each other:

in Irenaeus' words, noted in Chapter 4, 'the glory of God is a human *being fully alive*'.

In practice, being fully alive, in Paul's view, means reflecting God's own character, and that means living by faith, hope and love, though as the apostle emphasizes, the greatest of these three is love (1 Corinthians 13.13).

Other things follow about 'the church of God'. The Church is not in competition with any other human grouping. Like God, it has no enemies, or at least, it prays for those who so regard themselves, and so there is no question of the Church gaining at the expense of other human beings. In Egypt, Nigeria and elsewhere, it might seem that Christianity and Islam are in competition with each other, but this would be a serious misreading of the situation, and of the Bible, especially the New Testament.

The greatest contribution of St Paul to the well-being of the human race has yet to be realized: his passionate conviction that the God who crosses all boundaries is the friend of all, the enemy of none.

The God Who Crosses Boundaries in Acts

The author of the Acts of the Apostles has important things to say about God's purposes in history and his presence throughout the world. God's Holy Spirit plays a key role, and 'spirit', in both the Hebrew and Greek languages, could also mean 'breath', as in Genesis 2.7:

>...the Lord God formed man from the dust of the ground, and breathed into his nostrils the breath of life.

When God withdraws his 'breath', everything dies (Psalm 104.29). In the New Testament this all-pervasive Spirit (a 'You' rather than an 'It'), is now revealed as the Spirit of Jesus (Acts 16.7), bringing fullness of life.

The author of Acts is interested in the geographical range of the Holy Spirit, foreshadowed in the Pentecost story of 2.1-11. But why *Holy* Spirit? Above all, because it's *God's* Spirit, but also because, like 'the Holy One of Israel' of Isaiah 40–55, God's Spirit ranges far and wide, recognizing no boundaries, with no place off-limits. Yet God's Spirit remains holy — uncontaminated, as when 'the holy one of God' healed lepers (e.g. Luke 17.11-19), or when the Spirit was given even to 'unclean' Gentiles (Acts 10.44-45).

So, like the God in whom Paul came to believe, God's Spirit in Acts crosses boundaries, builds bridges between people of different races and backgrounds (2.1-11), and builds communities of friends (2.43-47). Most of all, the Spirit leads apostles into new territory (Acts 8.26, 29; 10.19; 11.12; 13.2-4; 16.6-7; 19.22; 20.22).

5. Summary

Paul's conversion led him to an understanding of God centred on the crucified and risen Christ, and it was Christ, rather than Jerusalem, its Temple or the law of Moses, who was now the centre of his world.

In a divine 'exchange', Jesus shared our place, so that as he, now and for ever, shares God's place, we might also share the same divine glory.

This revelation of God in Christ is crucial in interpreting Paul's more explicit and difficult teaching about women, gay people and predestination. That teaching may not be as negative as it has been made out to be.

The Church, as God's 'new creation', is the beginning of a human re-grouping around the crucified Christ.

6. Looking Ahead

'Icons are holy pictures of Christ, Mary and the saints...inseparable from eastern Orthodox spirituality.'[11] The word 'icon' comes from the Greek *eikon*, a word Paul uses when he calls Jesus 'the image of God' (2 Corinthians 4.4; Colossians 1.15). But does Paul think of himself as an 'icon' of Christ? It seems so. He tells the Christians at Corinth to imitate him, as he imitates Christ (1 Corinthians 11.1). Many other passages in his writings point the same way — for example, the parallels between himself and Jesus in Philippians (2.6-8; 3.4-11).

So, there's a lot to be said for the suggestion that Paul's word-portraits of himself as Christ's apostle reflect the heart of his understanding of God. If Christ reflects God, and Paul reflects Christ, that seems to be so.

Paul's self-portraits are full of contrasts and paradoxes. Paul is foolish, weak, disreputable; the worldly-wise Corinthians are wise, strong and honoured. He is like 'the rubbish of the world' (1 Corinthians 4.10, 13). He carries around in his own body 'the death of Jesus' so that 'the life of Jesus' can be seen there as well (2 Corinthians 4.10). He and his fellow-apostles are treated as 'sorrowful, yet always rejoicing; as poor, yet making any rich; as having nothing, and yet possessing everything'

(2 Corinthians 6.10). In yet another cameo, Paul's 'thorn in the flesh' must have been a serious physical affliction; there are echoes of the story of Job here (2 Corinthians 12.6-10).

So here, it seems, is a man who, faced by the suffering of God and of the world, has opted for compassion and sacrifice, rather than purity and religious aggression, his only 'boast' the cross of Jesus Christ (Galatians 6.14) or — in later parlance, a crucified God. In the end, I believe, this is where a Christian response to 'the problem of suffering' begins and ends.

✳ ✳ ✳

Three Questions for Reflection and Discussion

1   Was the biggest change in Paul the change from persecuting to suffering? If so, what is the different understanding of God behind this change?

2   Paul's new understanding of God is full of paradox: 'God's weakness...stronger than human strength', 'power...made perfect in weakness' etc. (1 Corinthians 1.25; 2 Corinthians 12.8; see also 2 Corinthians 6.3-10). Do we find parallels in our own or other people's experience?

3   Is the Church of God (Christ) really not in competition with any other human grouping? Not even 'rival attractions' on Sundays?

Going Deeper: Further Reading

Morna D. Hooker, *The Living Paul: A Short Introduction* (One World, 2003).

Neil Richardson, *Paul for Today* (Epworth/SCM, 2008).

Anthony C. Thistleton, *The Living Paul: An Introduction to the Apostle and his Thought* (SPCK, 2009).

Endnotes

1   Most scholars think that 1 and 2 Timothy and Titus were written by a disciple or later interpreter of Paul. Many take a similar view of Ephesians, Colossians and 2 Thessalonians.

2   Paul prefers the phrases 'in Christ' and 'in the Lord'. 'Christian' occurs only three times in the New Testament: Acts 11.26; 26.28 and 1 Peter 4.16.

3   The story of Paul's conversion is re-told twice in Acts (22.6-16; 26.12-18). 'Saul' becomes 'Paul', not at his conversion, but at Acts 13.9, as his travels begin.

4   Paul rarely alludes to Jesus' teaching and character: examples include 1 Corinthians 7.10; 9.14 and 11.23-26, and Philippians 2.5-11.

5   On Paul and God, see also the conclusion, 'Paul and the Question of God', in my *Paul for Today* (SCM, 2008), pp.190-99.

6   R. Dawkins, *The God Delusion* (Bantam, 2006), p.253.

7   Richardson, *The God Delusion*, p.87.

8   Romans 9.5 is ambiguous in the original Greek because of the lack of punctuation. Does Paul call Christ ('the Messiah') God here or not? (See the NRSV.)

9   See also 'What Paul didn't say about gay people', in Richardson, *The God Delusion*, pp.133-44.

10 On God's wrath, see also the discussions in Chapter 2, section 4, 'A Jealous God?', and Chapter 3, section 4, 'Wrath: God's Dark Side — or Ours?'.

11 *A Dictionary of Christian Spirituality*, ed. Gordon S. Wakefield (SCM, 1983), p.205.

7

'John's' Witness to God

'God is love' is the clearest 'lens' through which to view and to try make sense of the Bible as a whole.

Jesus is central to the New Testament's understanding of God, and Paul, as far as we know, was Jesus' leading interpreter in the early Church. But there was to be another hugely influential voice: that of 'John'. In fact, there are five New Testament writings associated with a 'John'.[1] In this chapter we shall look at

- John's Gospel, with its very distinctive 'take' on Jesus,

- the book of Revelation, asking how its often gruesome language and imagery fits into the overall biblical understanding of God,

- 'God in the End': New Testament teaching about the end of the world, and, finally,

- 1 John, which has a strong claim to be the climax of our exploration in this book.

1. 'John' and God

John's Gospel begins where Genesis began, but with a difference. Instead of 'In the beginning, God...', 'John' writes,

> In the beginning was the Word, the Word was with God, and the Word was God (John 1.1).

This, and the 17 verses which follow, set the scene for the entire Gospel. Like God (not an 'It', but a 'You'), when 'the Word' finally emerges into the light of history (1.14), the Word is a person, not an idea or a concept. But the word is still a word: a communication, as the conclusion to John's prologue shows:

> No one has ever seen God. It is God the only Son, who is close to the Father's heart, who has made him known (John 1.18; compare Hebrews 1.1).

So John sets out his stall. But we soon find that Jesus speaks differently in John. Gone are the parables we find in Matthew, Mark and Luke. No more 'Kingdom of God' language, apart from John 3.3 and 5. Jesus still talks about 'the Son of Man', but not in the same way as in the other Gospels. Above all, he talks about himself and 'the Father' or 'my Father'.

In the other Gospels Jesus was more reticent or cryptic about his own identity. The reader is left in no doubt that Jesus is the Son of God (Matthew 2.15; 3.17; Mark 1.1 etc.), but Jesus himself hardly ever talks about himself as the Son, and even then it's not clear whether anyone, even the disciples, hears these words:

All things have been handed over to me by my Father; and no one knows the Son except the Father, and no one knows the Father except the Son and anyone to whom the Son chooses to reveal him (Matthew 10.27; Luke 10.22).

But much of John's Gospel reads like an extended commentary on this verse, as I hope to show.

Spitting Image: Father and Son

In John, Father and Son are so close that on one occasion the Jesus of John actually says, 'The Father and I are one' (John 10.30; compare 17.21-22). To honour the Son is to honour the Father (5.23), and *vice versa*; to see the Son is to see the Father (12.45; 14.9); the glory of one is the glory of the other (13.31-32), and so on. This is Jesus' major theme in John's Gospel: Father and Son are 'hand in glove' — and even more than that: they are 'one'.

But they are not only 'one'; they are also, in some mysterious way, distinguishable, like God and 'the Word' 'in the beginning' (1.1). Jesus can even say, 'The Father is greater than me' (John 14.28). What is going on? What does it all mean?

John's Gospel was probably the last of the four to be completed, making more explicit, in his view, the identity and significance of Jesus. God sent Jesus (3.16 etc.), and there is an 'all or nothing' character about this mission. 'Either Jesus was speaking the truth in what he said about God or he was not.'[2]

This Gospel is teasingly like and unlike the others. Jesus is as controversial as ever — but more because of what he says about himself than because of the company he keeps. The same fate awaits him in Jerusalem — the same story is told, but with a difference. In an extra-ordinary paradox, the crucified Jesus in John dies in triumph. His last words are not a despairing prayer, as in Mark and Matthew, but a shout — or gasp — 'It's done!' (John 19.30).

The key to what these words mean lie is in an earlier verse:

> Now before the festival of the Passover, Jesus knew that his hour had come to depart this world and go to the Father. Having loved his own who were in the world, he loved them to the end (13.1).

One scholar described this verse as a headline for the rest of the book. The original Greek certainly suggests a link with Jesus' last words on the cross in this Gospel (*telos*, 13.1; *tetelestai*, 19.30). The triumph of Jesus, then, seems to be his 'success' in loving 'his own' until his very last breath.

The Hour of Glory

But John introduces two other important words into his distinctive 'take' on the death of Jesus. One is the word 'hour', as in 'My hour has not yet come' (e.g. 2.4) and 'The hour has come for the Son of Man to be glorified' (12.23). 'Glorify', along with 'glory', is John's other special word, which he uses to explain how he sees the death of Jesus. So, the prayer of Jesus just before his arrest begins,

> Father, the hour has come; glorify your Son so that the Son may glorify you... (John 17.1).

If we put these verses together, they seem to mean that the death of Jesus on the cross was his victory in loving 'to the end' *and* the revelation both of his glory and the glory of his Father. So, the glory of God is, above all, God's love. John's prologue anticipates this. There God's glory is defined by two things: 'grace and truth' (1.14), Old Testament words meaning the generous love of God, and his faithfulness in keeping his promises.

So John, like Paul, finds the heart of the revelation in, of all things, a crucifixion. Whereas Paul sees in it 'the weakness and foolishness of God' (1 Corinthians 1.25), John sees in it God's glory, the other side of the same coin.

Go-Between God

'The Son of Man' is pivotal in the story about God which John has to tell. The Son of Man is the go-between linking heaven and earth (1.51); he descends from heaven and ascends back to heaven (3.13; 6.51, 53, 62). The cross is his finest hour — the hour of his glory and, like a victorious Olympian stepping on to the podium, his coronation:

…the Son of Man must be lifted up (3.14).

So, this is 'end-game': the Son's hour of glory, hour of triumph, hour of ascent back to heaven — all these things. The fact that John can variously call Jesus 'the Son of God', 'the Son of Man' and, most of all, just 'the Son' underlines his role as the 'go-between' linking earth and heaven.

What changes? According to John, the 'breath' or 'spirit' of God is given and experienced in a new way. The outgoing God who, in Genesis, made a world, has begun to re-make the world, and 'breathing' his Spirit into the small group commissioned to help in this task (20.19-23).

The Holy Spirit: Jesus' 'Double'

The Spirit of God in John, however, is much more than a resource for the mission of the Church. The Spirit is Jesus' 'double' or *alter ego*. So, as with God and the Word, the language moves bewilderingly from Jesus to the Spirit and back again — as here:

> I will ask the Father, and he will give you another Advocate, to be with you forever. This is the Spirit of truth... You know him because he abides with you and he will be in you. I will not leave you orphaned; I am coming to you... (14.17-18).

Two themes provide the key to John's language about God. First, there is 'icon' language: the Spirit is Jesus' double, just as Jesus is 'the spitting image' of the Father. Second, there is language which can only be called the language of communion — a communion into which human beings are drawn:

> ...As you, Father, are in me and I am in you, may they also be in us, so that the world may believe that you have sent me (17.21).

This is the language of intimate friendship, as John's Jesus says (15.13-15). But, as with every special relationship, there is more to it than just deciding or choosing, as if it were within humankind's gift to decide whether to become friends of God or not. The initiative is, as John keeps saying, 'from above', not 'from below'. Jesus came from God — and went back to God, inviting the human race to join him and, through his *alter ego*, 'the Spirit of truth', enabling them to do so.

Judgement: The Darkness of Illusion

It would be wrong to give the impression that John's teaching about God is all light and sunshine. It is not. The darkness is never far away. But the darkness is humankind's choice:

> ...this is the judgement, that the light has come into the world, and people loved darkness rather than light because their deeds were evil (3.19).

This helps to explain a paradox in this Gospel: Jesus judges no-one, and yet, by that very fact, Jesus judges everyone (John 8.15-16). Why? Because passing judgement on each other is one of humankind's favourite occupations (as we and our newspapers demonstrate only too well).

For John, the fundamental sin is turning your back on the truth. And the fundamental truth, if there really is a 'Creator', is that we were made by God, in God and for God. This is why this Gospel presents the choice as one between the light and life of truth, and the darkness and death of illusion and unreality.

The Divine 'I Am'

What God can be to humankind, if humankind opens itself to the truth, is well summarized in the so-called 'I am' sayings attributed to Jesus in this Gospel. Jesus says 'I am the bread of life' (6.35, 48), 'the light of the world' (8.12; 9.5), 'the door' (10.7, 9), 'the good shepherd' (10.14), 'the resurrection and the life' (11.25), 'the way, the truth and the life' (14.6), 'the true vine' (15.1).

The 'I am' of these sayings would probably have suggested to the John's first 'readers' — they would most likely have been listening, not reading — that the speaker here was divine. In the Graeco-Roman world this was how a god or goddess might speak. But to people with a Jewish background, 'I am' would probably recall the name of God in Exodus 3.14, 'I AM WHO I AM' (thus the NRSV). Compare the words John gives to Jesus at 8.58, 'Before Abraham was, I am'.

These days one of these 'I am' sayings — 'I am the way, the truth and the life' — is especially controversial, and we must take a moment to look at this.[3] It is followed by

No-one comes to the Father except by me (14.6).

It is a pity, even tragic, that these words have become a biblical grenade for Christians to throw at people of other faiths. Every text has a context, and this verse is no exception. Jesus is talking to his anxious, despondent disciples here, not to people of other faiths. It is possible, in the light of later controversies, that these words were understood to exclude 'Christians' who thought that they could bypass the crucified Jesus and still reach God (1 John 4.1-6). But those verses in 1 John also have their context; the writer has in mind *Christians* who, in his view, were seriously distorting the faith.

If God is always and everywhere a mysterious 'three' — Father, Son and Holy Spirit — that casts an important retrospective light on the revelation mediated through the Old Testament, and perhaps further afield still. (See the further discussion in section 6, 'Looking Ahead', below.)

John's Gospel and Later Beliefs

New Testament writers rarely, if ever, say 'Jesus is God' in so many words. But John comes as near as any. Like Matthew, topping and tailing his Gospel with 'Immanuel' (1.23) and the divine 'I am with you' (28.20), John brackets his Gospel with '...the Word was God' (1.1), and the confession of the disciple Thomas before the risen Christ, 'My Lord and my God' (20.28). The 'I am' sayings of Jesus, discussed above, point the same way. This Gospel writer makes much more explicit what later centuries were to call 'the divinity' of Christ. Arguably, he takes the humanness of Jesus for granted. There are occasional, startling details such as a tired, thirsty Jesus (4.6-7), though later verses come close to suggesting that Jesus doesn't need food as ordinary mortals do (4.31-32). The shortest verse in John's Gospel, however, gives us someone unmistakably human: 'Jesus wept' (11.35).

So, John's Gospel lays the foundations for the later doctrine of the incarnation: the belief that Jesus was fully human and divine, truly human, truly God. I have argued throughout this book that God and humans in the Bible are never, as it were, competing for the same 'space', as if the more human the less divine and *vice versa*. Now, in this person Jesus, the stories of God and humankind converge. But it was God who initiated what this Gospel calls a mission of love to his world:

For God so loved the world that he gave his only Son... (John 3.16).

In a similar way, John's Gospel helps to pave the way for the Church's later conviction about God's essential 'three-ness', the doctrine of the Trinity. In this Gospel, as we have seen, the Son is 'the double' of the Father, and the Spirit 'the double' of the Son — an early anticipation of the later doctrine.

2. Still a Violent God?
The Book of Revelation

Many Christians tip-toe round the last book of the New Testament, or pretend it isn't there. A passage or two from Revelation thought suitable for a funeral service is quite enough for most tastes. The lectionaries used in churches around the world each Sunday seem to join the conspiracy in airbrushing out of sight the ugliest book of the New Testament (as it is often thought to be).

They have a point. The suffering and violence which God unleashes on the world in chapters 6–20 of Revelation are horrendous. No wonder the Church took a long time to decide that Revelation should be part of its scriptures, or that down the centuries voices such as Martin Luther's have advocated its exclusion from the Bible. On the other hand, churches which face persecution for their faith, like the churches for whom Revelation was first written, look more kindly on the last book of the New Testament.

Why the Book of Revelation Matters

I want to argue here for a more positive view of this book. Thomas Merton, twentieth-century Cistercian monk and popular writer, believed that we are living through the greatest crisis in the history of human-kind.[4] Richard Bauckham, distinguished New Testament scholar, has written of the importance of Revelation in renewing our doctrine of God, which he calls 'the most urgent contemporary theological need'.[5]

Unfortunately, a minority of Christians give Revelation a bad name by finding in its cryptic text hidden messages for our time. There was a spate of these in Britain some years ago by people convinced that the author of Revelation had the European Union in his sights. Nevertheless, this book has enormous relevance for today. It has far more references to 'the earth' than any other New Testament book, and so, belonging as we do to a generation bidding fair to destroy the earth, we would do well to pay attention to this difficult book.

Revelation in its Own Day

Revelation was a document of its time in three important ways. To appreciate these will help us understand where the author 'was coming from' in what he says about God.

First, Revelation belonged to a literary type which scholars call *apocalypses*. The book of Daniel in the Old Testament is one; Mark 13 has been called 'the little apocalypse', and apocalypses in general a 'literature of crisis'. They were written for people of faith in extreme situations. So, not surprisingly, their language can be extreme. Violent situations generate strong, if not violent, emotions. Authors of apocalyptic write powerfully about the judgements and justice of God in history.

Second, writers of apocalypses used what seems to us bizarre imagery — and often coded language — to interpret for the faithful the crisis they found themselves in. Much of this imagery had a history — necessarily so, otherwise its intended readers (or listeners) wouldn't have understood it. Revelation is steeped in the language and imagery of the Old Testament, and of the books of Ezekiel, Daniel and Zechariah in particular.

Appreciating this imagery is like learning a new language. Hebrew imagery 'appealed to the ear rather than the eye'.[6] For example, the picture of 'a figure like a man' — i.e. Jesus — with a sharp, two-edged sword coming out of his mouth (1.16) recalls modern surrealist art rather than an icon to be placed in a church. But the words were meant to be *heard*. Revelation's imagery can't be taken literally; it has to be read imaginatively — and seriously, as befits literature intended for a crisis.

Third, John, the author of Revelation, is a sharp observer of the contemporary scene: its power structures, the alluring propaganda of power, its injustice and violence. He knows what is going on. This is why Revelation is so subversive.

God and Jesus in Revelation

So what does Revelation say about God? Apparently, God has engaged in some 'power-sharing': God now shares his heavenly throne with 'the Lamb' — i.e. Jesus. (Paul's language about Jesus as Lord points the same way — Chapter 6, section 2, 'Jesus: In Our Place and in God's Place'.) John doesn't actually call Jesus 'God', but his language and imagery imply as much. People in Revelation worship both God *and* the Lamb (e.g. 5.13; 7.10). He also describes a figure 'like a man' (1.13-15), but with details (e.g. his hair; see Daniel 7.9) borrowed from Daniel's picture of the 'Ancient of Days' — i.e. God. This Lamb is the Jesus who was crucified, since he bears the marks of 'slaughter' (5.6). Even more strikingly, this Lamb has been slaughtered 'from the foundation of the world' (13.8). So, this is no new power-sharing agreement by God; it's just that it has only now been revealed.

There seems to be a contradiction here. How can a God who shares his throne with a slaughtered lamb be as violent as God is in chapters 6–20 of this book? I suggest (and others have argued this way), that we interpret the violent section of Revelation in the light of the less violent, more positive sections which encase it (chapters 1–5 and 19–22). For example, the image of Christ the warrior which dominates some of the middle chapters gives way to the image of Christ the bridegroom:

the marriage of the Lamb has come (19.7).

This is an important development, brought about, it seems, by the fall of 'Babylon' (i.e. Rome) in chapter 18. Until then, until God rights what is wrong in the world, 'the inhabitants of the earth' will have much to endure. In all of this, John was being realistic about the kind of world he lived in.

The Sovereignty of God

There are two things for us to keep in mind as we look, first, at God's sovereignty, and then at God's justice in Revelation. First, extreme situations generate extreme language. I shall not try to justify all the brutal-sounding, gruesome language of, say, Revelation 19.20 (though I shall return to the difficult subject of eternal punishment in the next section of this chapter). A second, crucial point is this: will evil, oppressive power-brokers have the last word in a world which they are wrecking? If they will, what remains of God's sovereignty and justice? This was the crisis in which John found himself.

The word 'apocalypse' comes from the Greek word meaning 'revelation'. So, John 'reveals' that, despite appearances, it is God, not Caesar, who really reigns. Crucially, God is Christlike: he shares that reign with 'the Lamb'. So, this imagery points in the direction of the Gospels, in which Mark 13, 'the little apocalypse' (and its parallels in Matthew and Luke) conveys the same message: God reigns. And that is, or should be, good news for everyone who wants to see a more just and peaceful world.

The Justice of God

What of God's justice in Revelation? We encounter it in the cry of the martyrs in heaven:

> Sovereign Lord, holy and true, how long will it be before you judge
> and avenge our blood on the inhabitants of the earth? (6.9).

The words sound vengeful, but, as one commentator suggests, this may be a call for public justice, not private revenge. After all, what can the sovereignty of God mean to people tortured in tyrants' prisons, or people deprived of home and livelihood by ruthless logging companies in Amazonian Brazil, if the evil they suffer will never be overthrown?

Modern Britons and Americans may be tempted to look kindly on the Roman Empire because of our own empires. Surely the Roman Empire was a good thing because ours was or is? We delude ourselves on both counts. The fact remains that, though much of the second century was to be less turbulent and violent than the first, Rome's heavy-handed rule, the appalling poverty of the many, in contrast to the luxurious living of the tiny minority in power, and the idolatry of attributing divine honours

to Caesar — all help to explain why the first Christians looked for a new
world order. Hence the triumphant climax of Revelation 18:

> Fallen, fallen is Babylon the great!
> It has become a dwelling place of demons... (v.2a)

God's Violence

So how do we explain all the destructiveness and violence attributed to
God in Revelation? To take one of the first examples in the book: the four
horsemen (6.1-7) unleash war, famine and pestilence. (The precise cost of
food staples given in v.6 might mean this is part-commentary on what
John could see happening.) As always with apocalyptic imagery, we must
take it seriously though not literally, looking for truth behind the
imagery. It is a commentary on the suffering and evil entailed by the
world's injustices and idolatries — as always in the Bible, the two go
together.

All of this is not what God inflicts or even 'allows', if that implies that
God could easily intervene, but chooses not to. It's better understood as
the awful emptiness and darkness which ensue from human beings'
exclusion of God. It is a picture similar to that in Romans 1.18-32: a
downward spiral, leading from idolatry into moral darkness and social
disintegration. But darkness is not the last word in Revelation. (We look
briefly at Revelation 21 and 22 in the next section of this chapter.)

Finally, we should recognize that Revelation doesn't have a monopoly
on divine violence in the New Testament — nearly, but not quite. The
author of Acts seems to interpret the sudden deaths of Ananias and
Sapphira and of Herod Agrippa as divine punishments (Acts 5.1-11;

12.21-24). Whatever historical facts lie behind these stories — Josephus, the Jewish historian, attributes Agrippa's death to natural causes — we must surely say, as with the Old Testament, that the 'real' God and the 'God' of the text are not the same.

3. God in the End

When we try to talk about life beyond this life and beyond our time-space continuum, we're trying to put into words what is beyond words. Just as we can't probe behind the origin of everything, so we can't peer beyond the end either. So, the word 'eternal' (*aionios* in the Greek), occurring over 60 times in the New Testament, is important. *Aionios* comes from the word *aion*, meaning 'age' — as in 'the age in which we live'. But the 'age' about which the New Testament speaks is 'the age to come'. So, 'eternal life' comes to mean 'the life of the age to come'. Like 'the kingdom of God', it refers to the life of God which God wishes to share with humankind.

People may begin to experience this eternal life here and now. 'John' says this most clearly (e.g. John 3.36; 1 John 5.11-12), but other writers say it, too. It is John also who clearly says what eternal life is: the knowledge of God and of Jesus, sent by God (17.3). It is a life which bridges even death. But what does this mean about the future, ours and the world's? And does the New Testament teach that this 'eternal life' is for all, or just for some? And if only for some, what about the rest?

Eternal Love and 'Punishment'?

The words and images of the New Testament about life after death and the end of the world are bewilderingly varied. (See the earlier discussion in Chapter 5, section 3, 'Not a God for Religious People'.) Some are fiercely negative, with, for example, two explicit references to 'the punishment of eternal destruction' (2 Thessalonians 1.9, compare Jude 7). ('Penalty', referring to the consequences of decisions made or actions taken, may be a better translation than 'punishment' here.)

But there is a lot more bleak language in the New Testament. Paul writes of people 'perishing' (significantly, always in the present tense, e.g. 1 Corinthians 1.18). John in Revelation, whilst reserving his severest language for the supernatural enemies of God, such as 'the dragon', refers to eternal 'torture' (14.9-11). My list of the New Testament's bleak language could go on.

Most twenty-first-century readers of the Bible will be disturbed, if not revolted, by language like this. Christian thinking about this has changed radically. A twentieth-century theologian speaks for many when he writes:

> ...we utterly reject the idea of a hell where God everlastingly punishes the wicked... Even earthly penologists are more enlightened nowadays.[7]

Whilst we can't be sure what exactly the biblical writers meant by their language, it is powerful and urgent, the language of extremity and crisis. Similarly, we might say of some dreadful situation, 'It was hell'. ('The hell' of utter loneliness and boredom is also relevant here.)

So what are we to make of all this scary language? Here we must anticipate the last section of this chapter: God is love. If, as the Bible says, that was or is really true, then it will always be true. God, being God, is consistent: true to God's own nature. But that doesn't preclude 'judgement'. As St John of the Cross wrote, 'In the evening of our lives we shall be examined in love'. It is the implication of the two great commandments: to love God 'with all our heart' and our neighbour 'as ourselves'.

To be examined in love might seem to some all too easy, as if, when the examiner is a friend of yours, there is no way you can fail. The New Testament is far more searching than this. 'Fire' is a recurring image of judgement, as in the teaching of Jesus. (On this see Chapter 5, section 2, 'The Strange Things Jesus Said about God'.) And if indeed God is love, that, I think, must mean God does not coerce. So, as the Russian writer Nicolas Berdyaev says, God can't violate human liberty; human beings are free to choose or not to choose happiness in God.

Even that isn't the end of the matter, since choice in human life isn't exactly a level playing-field. It's difficult to believe that Love gives up, even with their deaths, on people who in this life never had a chance. But that question takes us beyond the scope of this book.

End of the World?

There is also a cosmic scenario about judgement in the Bible. Will God obliterate the world because of its wickedness? The writer of 2 Peter[8] seems to have believed that (2 Peter 3.10, though the translation here is not certain). But, just as we can't take literally the details of the creation stories in Genesis, so here. That doesn't mean this verse becomes irrelevant. The future of a world threatened by nuclear weapons and climate change can't be taken for granted any more. So, 'will then God start somewhere else?'[9]

New Testament writers speak of the revelation or coming of Christ at the end (but not his 'second coming' — a later expression). A verse from Daniel, found on the lips of Jesus in the Gospels, is an example:

> Jesus said... 'You will see the Son of Man seated at the right hand of the Power' and 'coming with the clouds of heaven' (Mark 14.62).

Paul and Matthew's Gospel sometimes use the Greek word *parousia* (e.g. 1 Thessalonians 2.19; Matthew 24.3), which can mean both 'coming' and 'presence'. So, the Christ who will 'come' at the end is the Christ who is already present.

Behind all this (to us) strange language, the underlying conviction seems to be this: the God who is like Jesus will 'win out' in the end. Images and pictures in the Bible of the world's end vary, but the theme of God's final victory is common to them all. In the New Testament, God 'shares' the end with Jesus. Just as 'the Word' was there at the beginning, just as 'the Lamb' shares God's throne in heaven, so he will share God's triumph at the end (e.g. Philippians 2.9-11).

God and Humankind in the End

Many Christians today are unsure what they should believe about the future. That is hardly surprising, given the state of the world, the predictions of science and the difficulty of interpreting the New Testament. Biblical writers are trying to express the inexpressible: the merging of heaven and earth, the invisible and the visible, the transformation of this world into the world to come. Paul's words convey the heart of the matter: God will be 'all in all' (1 Corinthians 15.28). Two connected themes in the New Testament, however, are important.

First, St Paul suggests that that final triumph won't (can't?) occur without human beings:

> For the creation waits with eager longing for the revealing of the children of God (Romans 8.19).

God shares the end, not only with Jesus, but with 'all his saints' (1 Thessalonians 3.13). That may sound elitist, but the Bible springs surprises; both 'the sheep' and 'the goats' in Matthew 25.31-46 seem to have been surprised. The writer of 2 Peter urges his readers to work to hasten the day of the Lord (3.11). This comes close to what a modern Christian has written:

> Only a Christianized human race and cosmos can give eternal expression to the Church's universal character.[10]

Last but not least, a distinguished commentator on Revelation has remarked how generous the writer's final picture of the new Jerusalem is in chapters 21 and 22. True, there are exclusion clauses (21.7; 22.11), which should be interpreted in the light of the New Testament as a whole. But present in the new Jerusalem are 'the kings of the earth' (21.24), erstwhile opponents of God (19.19). In language reminiscent for us of the opening ceremony of a modern Olympic Games, into this city 'people will bring…the glory and honour of the nations'. Most hopeful of all, there is, as there was at the beginning of the Bible (Genesis 2.9), a tree of life. Here, at the Bible's end, its leaves are 'for the healing of the nations' (22.2).

4. The Bible's Climax:
The First Letter of John

Three letters, as well as a Gospel, carry the name 'John' in the New Testament. The name is not in the original documents, and represents, probably, the early Church's own detective work as it decided who wrote what.

Did a John write them? We can't know for sure, since 'the disciple whom Jesus loved' (e.g. John 13.23-25) is anonymous. Did the same person write both the Gospel and the letters? Probably not, because there are differences. Yet the Gospel and 1 John, especially, have the same distinctive voice, and 1 John provides a fitting finale to the Gospel.

> Beloved, let us love one another, because love is from God; every-one who loves is born of God and knows God. Whoever does not love does not know God, for God is love. God's love was revealed to us in this way: God sent his only Son into the world so that we might live through him (1 John 4.7-9).

This, I suggest, is the clearest 'lens' through which to view and to try to make sense of the Bible as a whole. 'God is love' can easily be senti-mentalized, but that would be a misunderstanding. God's love is humanity's life and judgement. 'Unbelief, by shutting the door on God's love, turns his love into judgement. For this is the meaning of judgement, that man [sic] shuts himself off from God's love.'[11]

Yet even 'God is love' can be misinterpreted, if we take 'God' to be 'a supernatural being'. I argued in the Introduction that that is an inadequate understanding of what 'God' means. God is not another entity, however great, additional to, or beyond, other entities. So, 'God *is* love' means just that. It doesn't mean 'God is a being who loves'. That easily leads to other statements about God which qualify love: for example, 'God loves, but must punish sin' etc. If God *is* love, everything about God must be understood in that light. In the mystery of God's being there is nothing at all which is other than, or contradictory to, love.

I have chosen to end my all-too-brief survey of the Bible because I am convinced that 'God is love' is the key to the biblical understanding of God. All that precedes and follows must be seen in the light of this verse. That doesn't mean that the Bible's enormously rich and varied language about God should be flattened out into a 'strap-line' which would quickly become a sentimental cliché. 'Love' is over-used in Christian pulpits as it is. It all too easily becomes a substitute for serious thinking about more difficult biblical ideas and language.

As we have seen, there are plenty of such difficulties in the Bible: violence in plenty attributed to God, together with references to God's 'wrath' and 'jealousy'. But love is still the key. The Bible's purpose, after all, is to help people to fulfil the two great commandments: to love God and our neighbour. And, for all the difficulties of its final book, it points to a final victory of Love.

5. Summary

John's Gospel carries on where the other Gospels left off. It unpacks what the author believed to be Jesus' deepest identity: son of the Father. It equates God's glory with God's love, applies, more than other writers, exalted language of divinity to Jesus, and invites disciples, through 'the Spirit of truth', to be where Jesus himself is, 'in the Father'.

The God of Revelation, like the God of other biblical writings attributing violence to God, can't be simply identified with God as God really is. But Revelation carried — and still carries — a powerful message about God's sovereignty and justice in critical times.

New Testament pictures of the End offer the hope of an ultimate victory of a Christlike God. But a God who is love cannot or will not coerce — hence its dire warnings.

1 John's message that 'God is love' has good claim to be the climax of, and the key to, the Bible, casting a retrospective light over the whole.

6. Looking Ahead

I suggested at the end of Chapter 5 that the so-called 'doctrine of the Trinity' — the Christian belief in the three-in-oneness of God (Father, Son and Holy Spirit) — was the outcome of where the Bible begins: an outgoing God who made a world. 'God is love' (1 John 4.8, 16) anticipates that doctrine of the Trinity, better thought of as a new experience and understanding of God. It was a 'revelation' which embraced and transformed people. The death and resurrection of Jesus were, from the beginning, seen as the climax and heart of that revelation.

So what does the Bible say, or imply, about people of other faiths? I return to the earlier discussion of a verse in John's Gospel:

> Jesus said to him (sc. Thomas), 'I am the way, the truth and the life. No one comes to the Father except through me' (John 14.6).

In view of what this Gospel has said earlier about the Father and the Son — they are 'one' (10.30) — this should not surprise us: how could there be another route to the heart of God except 'through' the Son?

Unfortunately, many Christians paraphrase 'except through me' in an exclusive sense: '…unless you become a Christian'. But the words don't say this. It is something we read into them. They are not so much laying down a condition which effectively excludes Muslims and others who have, like as not, never had the opportunity to embrace the Christian faith anyway; they are simply expressing the reality of love: the Father and the Son are 'one'.

What this verse doesn't say is whether the God who is eternally Father, Son and Holy Spirit has revealed himself in other places and times, and in other ways. Christians have no grounds for being dogmatic about this, even though most will want to hold on to — as I do — their 'hunch' that there is a uniqueness about Jesus — as the New Testament claims.

This century is, increasingly, the time for courteous, open conversations with people of other faiths. 'Open' here does not imply a relativist view, as if there are no real differences between faiths. But they are still not rivals or competitors, even though many people, Christians included, often see it like that.

Truth is one — how could it be otherwise if there is one 'Creator' of all things? But we would do better to start living the truth before we start to assert it, and to live the reality of John 14.6, rather than lob it like a hand-grenade into the middle of an inter-faith discussion. In John's own terms, 'abiding in the Father and the Son' means, first and foremost, living in and by the love of the God who is love.

* * *

Three Questions for Reflection
and Discussion

1   Do you agree that 'God is love' is the key to the whole Bible? If so, what are the implications? And if not, what are the implications?
2   Can New Testament language about the end — ours and the world's — illumine life now?
3   Is talk about 'the uniqueness' of Jesus true? If true, is it helpful or unhelpful in a time of increasing inter-faith contact and discussion?

Going Deeper: Further Reading

Neil Richardson, *John for Today* (SCM, 2010).

Christopher Rowland, *Revelation* (Epworth/SCM, 1993).

Stephen H. Travis, *Christ and the Judgement of God* (Paternoster/ Hendrickson, 2009).

Endnotes

1   We know a 'John' wrote Revelation because he tells us (Revelation 1.3, 9). On the authorship of the Gospel and Letters of 'John', see the introductory paragraph to section 4 of this chapter.
2   N. Richardson, *John for Today* (SCM, 2010), p.30.
3   On John 14.6, see also Richardson, *John for Today*, pp.76-83.
4   T. Merton, *Contemplation in a World of Action* (Unwin Paperbacks, 1965).

5   R. Bauckham, The Theology of the Book of Revelation (Cambridge, 1993), p.164.

6   J. Sweet, *Revelation* (SCM, 1979), p.14.

7   J. Macquarrie, *Principles of Christian Theology* (SCM, 1966), p.327.

8   Many biblical writings, or sections of them, in keeping it seems with conventions of the time, carry the name of prophets and apostles, even though they didn't write it all, or even any of it.

9   The question of one of my readers, Dr Stan Pearson. (See the acknowledgements in the Foreword.)

10   N. Berdyaev, *Freedom and the Spirit* (Geoffrey Bles, the Centenary Press, 1935), p.348.

11   Richardson, *John for Today*, p.31, quoting R. Bultmann.

Summary of Summaries

The first book of the Bible introduces us to the story of God and the story of human beings, creatures who reflect God's own capacity for creativity, relationships and promise-making, and who are entrusted with a pivotal role in God's world. The story of the human 'fall' is not about our freedom to choose, but our unfulfilled potential for partnership with God and the freedom and maturity which goes with that.

The stories of God's destructiveness in Genesis should not be understood literally. Their sequels — the rainbow and the call of Abraham — suggest that God doesn't give up easily. Instead, God commits himself again to making a world — and that is clearly going to be 'a long haul' (Chapter 1).

Like the story of the Flood in Genesis, the stories of the Exodus from Egypt and the Conquest of Canaan are questionable on both historical and theological grounds. It's unlikely they ever happened, and no amount of special pleading can make acceptable the picture of God presented here. The 'God' of the text can't be identified with God as God really is, if we are to arrive at a consistent understanding of God in the very varied testimonies of the Bible.

A good example of biblical language which should not be taken literally is the phrase 'chariots and horses'. The phrase has an ideological function: that is, it typifies powers hostile to God. As for the 'jealousy' of God, despite the Old Testament's sometimes offensive imagery, it is a biblical theme which points up God's commitment to Israel, and, ultimately, God's passionate concern for the well-being of humankind (Chapter 2).

With the historical events of the destruction by Assyria and Babylon of Israel and Judah as independent nations we encounter more difficult biblical ideas about God. Although it was natural (in the understanding of the time) — and even necessary — to believe that these catastrophes were God's punishments of Israel ad Judah, it is not an explanation that we can easily accept. God doesn't 'run' the world like that, and the idea that the sun always 'shines on the righteous' began to be questioned then — and continues to be. But the crisis of faith of the Judaean exiles in Babylon, and the heart-searching which went with it, was to lead to a greater understanding of God and a wider vision of the world.

Yet even though we must question biblical ideas of divine punishment, the concept of God's 'judgement' — that contravening the moral order of God's world may bring disaster — is both important and necessary. A similar point needs to be made about God's 'wrath'. In seeking to understand this biblical theme, it may help to compare God's anger with human anger *at its best and most self-possessed*. It's a sign that someone cares (Chapter 3).

There are two particularly important 'God' words in the Old Testament. God is 'righteous' — utterly consistent in character, relationships and in keeping his promises — and God is also 'holy' — uniquely God, even when God involves himself in the world for the sake of his people Israel. God is a Reality who can't be compromised or contaminated.

It is misleading to think of God as God of the 'spiritual' only. The Bible doesn't usually distinguish between 'the spiritual' and the 'material' or 'physical' in the way that contemporary expressions of Christianity often do. God is God of the everyday, and the Bible surprisingly down-to-earth.

Yet God can be elusive, and life can be cruel, as Job found in the story which bears his name. This story candidly recognizes the theological problem posed by the suffering of a good man. In such a crisis of faith, pious clichés are out of place; a threatened, angry human being is 'allowed' to protest vigorously, as Job did.

Though all language applied to God is inadequate, God is a 'You' rather than an 'It', as the personal language of the Psalms amply demonstrates. God is both 'my God' and 'our God', the latter phrase, especially, being developed further in the New Testament in the light of Jesus (Chapter 4).

In the New Testament the resurrection is God's 'Yes' to Jesus; it casts God's confirming light over the life and even the death of Jesus. This is crucial to our understanding of both Jesus and God, because Jesus spoke and acted for an extraordinarily generous, disturbing God whose 'kingdom' was very near and into which the most unlikely people were invited. Jesus taught his disciples to address God in a way which would recall his own practice — as 'Father'. But Jesus was also a disturbing, iconoclastic presence — especially, it seems, to religious people — and it was to cost him his life.

All this, because of the resurrection, is why Jesus became central to the Christian understanding of God (Chapter 5).

Paul's encounter with the crucified and risen Christ on the Damascus road changed his understanding of God. His life's work was to take the gospel of Jesus to the Gentiles, and so to bear witness to a 'boundary-crossing' God. In letters to churches, he explored in depth the meaning of Jesus' death and resurrection. In a divine 'exchange', Jesus shared our place, and now and forever, as 'Lord', shares God's place as well, making possible our life 'in Christ'.

Paul's more culturally specific teaching — about women, and, in some respects, about same-sex relationships — need to be interpreted in the light of his understanding of God's revelation in Christ. His teaching on predestination (Romans 9–11, in particular) may also not be as narrow as some Christians believe. As for the Church, it is, above all, God's 'new creation': the beginning of a human re-grouping around the crucified Christ (Chapter 6).

John's Gospel carries on where the other Gospels leave off. It explores the meaning of Jesus' deepest identity as son of the Father, equating God's glory with God's love, and applying to Jesus, more than any other New Testament writer, exalted language of divinity. It invites its readers into a communion with God ('the Father') made possible by the Son and the Spirit.

The God of Revelation, like the God of other biblical writings attributing violence to God, can't be simply identified with God as God really is. But this last book of the Bible should not be ignored, especially today. It carries an urgent message about God's sovereignty and justice.

New Testament pictures of the End offer the hope of an ultimate victory of a Christlike God. But a God who is love cannot or will not coerce — hence their dire warnings.

Finally, 1 John's message that 'God is love' (1 John 4.8, 16) has good claim to be the climax of scripture, casting a retrospective light over the whole Bible. This is the key to the biblical understanding of God (Chapter 7).

Conclusion

The most important question the world faces is the question of God.

God is on the side of life...but...are we?

1. Gods

There are always gods. The gods may not be recognized or acknowledged; they may even be denied, but they are there. A god is never far away — that icon or centre on to which are projected (for example) a nation's purpose and values, and what it believes to be true.

There may be more than one god: different values, purposes and estimates of what really matters in life. In the words of Martin Luther, 'What your heart clings to and entrusts itself to is your god'. Some gods may be far from obvious; others seem perfectly 'natural': a person's family, for example. Some gods will have more power than others, even be in conflict with each other. But gods are still a fact of life.

Should they be called 'gods'? Perhaps not. But to call them 'gods' helps to expose them as impostors, since there is only one source of life, one Creator. An impostor god purports to give life, but it won't be life for all; it will be life for some at the expense of others. And it may be an illusory life. That is how 'gods' work — capitalism, for example, or the market.

Impostor gods appear to give life — a life of sorts — but they also drain life from their devotees, making them less human. (You live with an idol until you grow like it, according to Psalm 115.4-8.) Gods also require sacrifice, whether from their devotees or from others who do not belong to that favoured circle.

That is another mark of impostor gods. They divide; they do not unite — unless they are put in their place. Gods may have a place — a God-given place if they are part of creation, like sex or the family, or if they have a legitimate role to play in the world, like a nation. But gods are likely to run wild when they move from their God-given place and become the centre themselves.

You can often tell who or what has godlike status because a god is beyond question or criticism. It may be the nation; it may be its constitution or its values. It may be a religion, its Scriptures, a Church; a religious god, especially, should not be mistaken for the real God. The identifying mark is always the same: beyond criticism or question. ('If you start to question the Bible, where do you stop? What is there left to hang on to?')

You can tell a nation's gods by those assumptions, spoken or unspoken, which are beyond question. The mantras of political leaders help us identify a nation's gods: 'hard-working families', 'competing in the global race', 'the tax-payer'. Is this the language of a country whose gods are property and money, those central, defining values to which all else must be sacrificed?

They will deny that. But the presence of the poor suggests otherwise. The poverty and misery of people unable to work hard because they are too unwell, or to pay taxes because they are too poor testifies to the power of the gods. Their poverty shows there is a power in the land, draining the humanity out of its devotees. Where there are gods, there are always victims.

All substitute gods are fragile, as the psalmists of the Old Testament knew. They wield power, but it is a brittle power: a major crisis, a well-aimed criticism, and — suddenly — 'the emperor has no clothes'. Until, that is, people give this brittle god new power because it suits them to do so. Gods — unlike the real God — support vested interests; they need those vested interests in order to keep their godlike status.

There are always gods, and it matters supremely whether it's a god or God — the real and only source of ultimate value, truth and meaning in the life of the world. Only in this, the real God, is the human race likely to find its unity and peace.

2. The Real God

God — the real God — is not beyond criticism. Unlike the impostor gods, the real God does not disintegrate at the first question. God's devotees do not spring angrily or aggressively to God's defence at the first whiff of criticism. If they do, then they have confused their idol with the real God.

God — the real God — does not require victims or sacrifices. In the view of Christian faith, God was and is both sacrifice and victim; Jesus — his life, death and resurrection — is the reason for believing that. God is love, and love by nature is selfless and sacrificial. But there are no scapegoats, no punishments, no legal penalties.

The real God does not divide — despite the toxic distortions of Christianity prevalent in the world. (As I suggested in the Introduction, there is such a thing as 'Christian idolatry'.) The agenda of the real God is the unity, healing and peace of creation — the agenda, also, of humans who seek to reflect the mind and heart of the Creator.

According to the Bible, the real God 'is like no other'. This is not a tribal claim, since the real God is the Creator of all and cares for all. If any group makes such a claim ('Our god is a great big god'?), it is misguided, even when the 'tribe' is a Christian one. Between God and the gods, including Christian idols, a great gulf is fixed.

How may we know when we, or anyone else, are worshipping an idol? How can we be sure that we are in touch with 'the living God' (one of the Bible's descriptions of the real God), rather than a lifeless idol, even if that idol is described in Christian language? That very description provides the clue. The living God, the real God, makes people come alive, makes them more aware and self-aware, and especially more aware of other people. The real God makes them more compassionate and generous, less anxious and preoccupied.

For most people, this is a lifetime's work. But God's project is a human one: to unite nations with nations, people with people, and — inseparable from these hopes — the human race with their Creator.

Will one God be tolerant? Yes — deeply tolerant of human beings, though not of humans abusing or oppressing other humans. But God, the Creator out of whose power has come the world as we know it, is not merely tolerant. God has made human beings in God's own image. God affirms human life, cherishes it, nurtures it. And this is not narcissistic; love, by its very nature, is not narcissistic.

But is the Bible on the side of life? Many oppressed groups have wondered — and still do: slaves, women, the original inhabitants of lands colonized by Europeans...and people still oppressed by toxic forms of Christianity. It's a long list. This is why the Bible has to be read differently.

3. God and the 'God' of the Bible

Over the twenty or so centuries since it was born, the Christian faith has undergone many far-reaching changes and adaptations. New territories and cultures, new human knowledge and achievements, new insights and experience — all these have contributed to a mutating Christian faith. The Bible itself bears witness to a pattern of continuity and change.

So with the Bible: we must think about it and read it differently. Narratives in the past tense in the Bible cannot be read as straightforward historical accounts, or, sometimes, as historical accounts at all. (Contradictions in what are clearly versions of the same event are one indicator.) Even writings which look and sound historical are often a mix of memories edited and re-cycled. The Bible's language is not only or primarily historical; it is also theological, imaginative, ideological, rhetorical; fact and symbol, the literal and the metaphorical may alternate in bewildering fashion.

So we can no longer identify the 'God' of the text with the real God, and, given the dastardly deeds sometimes attributed to the God of the text (on this see Chapters 2, 3 and 7), we should be profoundly glad about this.

But 'Back to the Bible' can be a strident, powerful war cry. (War cry it usually is.) Such a call is nostalgic, emotive and misleading. 'Forward with the Bible' is better, but even that begs important questions. For example, who are the people whose slogan this has become? If there is a militant look in their eyes — then beware!

The Bible's purpose is simple: to help its readers and its hearers to fulfil its two great commandments: to love God with all our heart and our neighbour as a human being like ourselves. We should be suspicious of anything less or different. Reading the Bible with that aspiration will ensure that we don't read it like any other book.

But we need to look more closely at the relationship between the Bible and the real God. Even though the 'God' of the biblical texts can't be identified straightforwardly with the real God, there is still a vital connection.

4. God, Jesus and the Bible

In 'Interlude (2)' I suggested that the Christian faith should be thought of as the religion of a person rather than of a book. 'The book' plays a unique, indispensable role, but it is not as central as the person of Jesus. For Christians, Jesus is the key to the Bible. The Old Testament must be allowed its own voice, and not Christianized in a way which drowns out that voice. But from the beginning of the Church, Christians have hailed Jesus as the 'fulfilment' of the scriptures.

That doesn't mean the scriptures predicted him. It does mean that Jesus, in retrospect, can be seen to be the direction in which the scriptures were pointing. There are three steps in the argument here:

1 the 'God' of the Old and New Testament texts points to the real God;

2 Jesus' revelation of God is, for Christians, definitive;

3 Jesus, then, must be the key to the whole Bible.

5. God and Jesus

Jesus is the Christians' 'key' to interpreting that extraordinary jumble of stories, poems, commandments etc. which comprise the Bible. To mention just three Old Testament themes, Jesus is the key to the law, the wisdom of God and the coming liberator to whom many prophecies pointed. Jesus was also the catalyst who inspired those 27 writings which the Church eventually called 'the New Testament'.

So we turn to the Bible, though not exclusively to the Bible, to learn about Jesus, and we make Jesus the key to understanding it. The process is circular, but it's a creative, not a vicious circle.

The resurrection of Jesus was and is as much about God as about Jesus. The resurrection wasn't just an extraordinary miracle or a supernatural event. It was a revelation. The resurrection of Jesus is the Christian 'take' on belief in God:

the God who reaches us in and beyond suffering, evil and death, the God who works through the mess and tragedy of human history to heal our relationships with each other and with our Creator.

So, the resurrection is the meaning of the cross and of the life of which the cross was the climax. The resurrection was God's 'Yes' to Jesus, changing for ever how we should understand the words at the end of the Lord's Prayer,

Yours is the kingdom, the power and the glory.

Look at the life of Jesus, or eavesdrop on his teaching, if you want images of that kingdom. Look, paradoxically, at his dying, to grasp the paradox of the divine glory. As for power, I have not found anywhere a more illuminating paragraph than this:

God works not by power, in our understanding of that word, but by powerlessness. Certainly God has power, and by it God created the heaven and the earth… But what we know of God, both from the Bible and from our own experience, is that he does not work in his world by the exercise of power. God's 'power' refers to the nature of his being, his unlimited ability and resources, not to his way of operating. It is not, as with the human beings, the power of domination that forces people to do the will of God, but the hidden, mysterious power that works through weakness, as is seen in the Cross of Christ.[1]

God — the real God — chooses to lead his creation from — of all places — a cross. That is the mystery and the glory of Love.

6. The World's Future

Idolatry — worshipping what is less than God — has consequences, simply because creation is built that way. Creation has a way of reverting to chaos when it is abused. A powerful prophecy of Jeremiah is coming eerily true in the current ecological crisis:

> I looked on the earth, and lo, it was waste and void;
>
> and to the heavens, and they had no light...
>
> I looked...
>
> and all the birds of the air had fled.
>
> I looked and, lo, the fruitful land was a desert... (Jeremiah 4.23, 25, 26a).

In the words of one Old Testament scholar, 'The judgement of the world is evidently taking the form of a creeping death for the ecosystem of planet earth... We're all collectively responsible for the fate of the earth.'[2] The arid, polarized debate between creationists and evolutionists completely bypasses the real challenge of the Bible for today: will God's creation flourish in human hands, or be destroyed by them?

A great theologian, Karl Barth, pointed out that the last chapter of the Bible has 'a book of life', but not 'a book of death'. God is on the side of life. But which side are humans on? Nuclear weapons and the arms race, the pollution of the planet, the tobacco industry, our idolatry of profit and the oppression of the poor — all this and more puts a huge question-mark over humankind: are we for life or for death?

The Bible sows the seeds of an all-embracing humanism, a true internationalism, and even offers a basis for a searching, but always courteous, engagement between world faiths — an engagement deeper than the world has yet seen.

7. A God-Crisis and Belief in the Real God

I return to where we began. The most important question the world faces is the question of God: is there a Creator, and, if so, what is the character and purpose of that Creator? The answers we give to those questions affect so much else: world poverty, the arms race, the way we use the resources of the planet, not to mention our relationships with each other.

Many of us are not very good at speaking about God. Religious people can lapse into a confused, embarrassed silence. We don't know what to say in the face of the world's hostility and scepticism. At the other extreme, we can prattle on about God as if God were as obvious and as accessible as the kitchen sink. A professional Christian, as I have been through most of my adult life, can be especially guilty of this. God easily becomes the great patron of the Church who might, if we ask nicely, give us a sunny day for the church picnic. I caricature, but not unduly.

It's not surprising there is a God-crisis. On a day in September, 2001, nearly 3,000 people lost their lives as their killers said their prayers. 'Christian' nations responded in kind, unleashing a war on terror. Religious bullying at a personal level is only too plentiful: a gay teenager expelled from home by religious parents, children abused by people professing to believe in God... The list could go on.

There can easily be, in those of us who profess to believe in God, a disjunction between belief and life. Belief in God is more than ticking a box in a questionnaire about religion. But though some may keep a god like a top hat (G.K. Chesterton), wheeled out on 'high-days and holidays', belief in the real God is a far deeper affair.

But, in some ways, that's harder. God is easily missed — or marginalized — for many reasons. The crucifixion of Jesus of Nazareth invites us to believe that the Creator of all is both self-effacing and selfless, neither over-bearing nor even obvious. It may feel different on days when we are overwhelmed, for example, by the beauty of creation or of human life. But if God is real, then God has clearly given us space enough not to believe.

Arguments for the existence of God can only get us so far. But there is much to be said for the advice of George McLeod, founder of the Iona Community in Scotland. The way to belief in God, said McLeod, was to live *as if* God exists. And what would that involve? Perhaps something like this:

- to respond wholeheartedly and humanly to life in all its mystery and beauty, its problems, suffering and evil,

- to respond compassionately to our fellow-human beings,

- to engage as honestly as we can with ourselves,

- to live with a grateful heart.

Belief in God is not an easy call, but such a life, I believe, brings us close to the God who, in the crucified and risen Jesus, is revealed as Love.

* * *

Three Questions for Reflection and Discussion

1   Do you agree with the differences suggested here between 'gods' and 'the real God'?

2   'The New Testament lies hidden in the Old, and the Old is made plain in the New' (St Augustine — see Interlude [2]). Do you find St Augustine's view of the Bible convincing?

3   Is there a 'God-crisis' today, and, whether there is or not, what bearing do you think this has on the world's future?

Endnotes

1   A. Ryrie, *The Prayer of Silence* (SLG, 2012), p.83.

2   Erhard S. Gerstenberger, *Theologies in the Old Testament* (T. & T. Clark, 2002), pp.304-5.

A Personal Postscript

I became a Christian as a young teenager. I cannot now remember details of my adolescent faith, though I do remember being frightened of hell, and troubled when a teacher of mine put into my hands a book casting doubt on the resurrection of Jesus. *The Transforming Friendship*, a popular book by the Methodist preacher, Leslie Weatherhead, helped me to a more settled place, and my later teens were happier than my early teens had been.

In those years all my close friends at school were agnostics or atheists, and it is probably they who gave me a lasting interest in 'Christian apologetics', the technical term for explaining and defending the Christian faith to those who do not share it. I had much to learn; I'm not aware I made any converts.

Over half a century later, my understanding of the Bible has changed a great deal. I have learned to question the Bible in a way that my teenage self would never have dreamed of. Most of that half century I have spent as an ordained minister in the British Methodist Church, and much of my ministry teaching the Bible to ordinands. But I have also been a 'circuit' minister in Oxford, Manchester and Leeds, with two student chaplaincies along the way. So, this book is, in part, the outcome of nearly half a century of preaching and teaching.

But though my questions and even criticisms of the Bible have grown, so too my appreciation of it has deepened, as well as my own personal use of it. I don't doubt its authority and inspiration; in this book I've tried to set out what I mean by those words.

I'm sure my understanding of God has changed, too, though that is more difficult to track. If God exists (a rather bald way of expressing this mystery), then, by definition, God is an all-pervasive presence, and that remains a growing conviction. Yet there have been theological milestones in my journey, some intellectual, some more personal.

For example, I do not recall my younger self ever wondering if God suffered. But I have wrestled with that question for many years now. Much more important, I have learned from friends who suffer what I could not have learned from books. And they have helped me to understand the Bible better.

Another example: my understanding of hell has changed since that troubled spell in my teens. I continue to believe that hell is real, but not that a stern, unbending God sends there people who don't believe in God. I hope and trust that no-one can finally put him- or herself beyond the reach of God's love. But can any of us be dogmatic about that?

I have wondered, too, what the Bible means by the 'wrath' and 'judgement' of God. It is a tragedy that strident literalist readers of the Bible make the Bible incredible or offensive (offensive for the wrong reasons) to others.

God's 'wrath' isn't lightning strikes and thunderbolts, but the darkness which begins to descend on human life and human communities when we neglect the truth about ourselves, life and God. It's the darkness in which we find it difficult to distinguish illusion from reality, truth from propaganda, what really matters from what doesn't.

This is why I am convinced that belief in God — the real God — is so important for the future of the world. A former colleague, Henry McKeating (see Chapter 3), suggested to me once that one example of the darkness which the Bible calls God's 'wrath' is governments believing their own propaganda. Add to that contemporary obtuseness about nuclear threats and climate change, and the need for the light of God becomes urgent indeed.

But I prefer to end by writing about the love of God (though 'wrath' is love in disguise). I have learned so much about love from my marriage and my family — and still more, in these last few years, as a grandparent.

I'm grateful that I've lived my life thus far as one who believes in God. Like a good marriage, it gets better as time goes on. But belief in God doesn't get easier — any more than prayer does. Practice helps. But how could praying for others (for example) become easier — especially if we take seriously Jesus' commands to pray for 'enemies' *and* 'Do not judge'?

As for practising belief in God, I've come to the conclusion that that is crucial. Church comes into it — exasperating, attractive, off-putting, indispensable church — but it's far from the whole picture. I am learning from experience and from theologians that belief in God also involves putting more of ourselves into what we have to do each day, however humdrum or unpalatable that may be. It involves facing outwards, and reading human faces with understanding and compassion, as well as facing 'inwards' and being honest with ourselves. Best of all, it involves being open, as much as we can, to that Presence who is — unlike today's life-destroying impostors — the real God. This God is the personal reality whom Jesus of Nazareth leads me to believe *is* Love. But that's neither an easy call nor an easy conclusion.

Index of Biblical References